D1205007

DISCARDED

JEROME LIBRARY—BOWLING GREEN STATE UNIVERSITY

FORM AND CONTENT

Library of Philosophy and Logic

General Editors:
P. T. Geach, P. F. Strawson, David Wiggins, Peter Winch

FORM AND CONTENT

BERNARD HARRISON

OXFORD
BASIL BLACKWELL
1973

ISBN 0 631 15030 7

© Basil Blackwell 1973

Library of Congress Catalog Card Number
73—80195

All Rights Reserved. No part of this publication may be
reproduced, stored in a retrieval system, or transmitted,
in any form or by any means, electronic, mechanical, photo-
copying, recording or otherwise, without the prior permission
of Basil Blackwell & Mott Limited.

Printed in Great Britain by
Western Printing Services Ltd, Bristol
and bound by Kemp Hall Bindery, Oxford

FOR DOT

It is evident, that even different simple ideas may have a similarity or resemblance to each other; nor is it necessary that the point or circumstance of resemblance should be distinct or separable from that in which they differ. *Blue* and *green* are different simple ideas. but are more resembling than *blue* and *scarlet;* though their perfect simplicity excludes all possibility of separation or distinction. It is the same case with particular sounds, and tests and smells. These admit of infinite resemblances upon the general appearance and comparison, without having any common circumstance the same. And of this we may be certain, even from the abstract terms *simple idea*. They comprehend all simple ideas under them. These resemble each other in their simplicity. And yet from their very nature, which excludes all composition, this circumstance, in which they resemble, is not distinguishable or separable from the rest. It is the same case with all the degrees in any quality. They are all resembling, and yet the quality, in any individual, is not distinct from the degree.

David Hume, *Treatise of Human Nature*, Bk 1,
Part 1, VII, footnote

The *senses* have . . . become *theoreticians* immediately in their *praxis*.

Marx, *Economic and Philosophic Manuscripts* (1844)

Contents

Preface

The chief influences on this book are, as will be obvious, Wittgenstein—the early Wittgenstein as much as the late—and Noam Chomsky. I have profited as well from the conversation of many teachers and colleagues, including most recently T. L. S. Sprigg, A. D. Nuttall and Gabriel Josipovici.

I owe a particular debt of gratitude to Aaron Sloman and John Mepham, who read an earlier draft of the manuscript and discussed it with me at great length. If the book is less obscure and groping than it was in that version the credit is mainly theirs. I am also grateful to the University of Sussex for freeing me from teaching and most administrative duties in the Summer Term of 1970–1, during which most of the first draft was written.

A trial run of some of the ideas put forward here appears in *Inquiry* for 1967 under the title 'On Describing Colours'. A much fuller exposition of the theory of meaning presupposed by much of what I say here will be found in my book *Meaning and Structure*, published by Harper & Row.

Kingston near Lewes, Sussex
July 1972

PART 1
Naming and Discrimination

1. Naming and Discrimination

I

It is often held that language can express only the form but not the content of experience. I shall call this thesis 'the thesis of the inexpressibility of content' or 'the inexpressibility thesis' for short. I shall argue that on both the interpretations of it that are current in contemporary philosophy[1] it is false, and that its falsity on these interpretations has important epistemological consequences, particularly in connexion with scepticism about the content of the experience enjoyed by other minds. The two versions of the thesis that I have in mind are those put forward respectively by Moritz Schlick, in a discussion which is still, to my mind, the best on the topic in the literature of analytic philosophy[2] and more recently, by a number of writers including J. J. C. Smart[3] and B. A. Farrell.[4] I shall discuss the latter set of arguments first.

[1] Contemporary discussions have, I think, genuinely superseded traditional ones on this and related topics, so that we need not refer back, for example to Descartes' and Galileos' theories of primary and secondary qualities or to Locke's distinction between simple and complex ideas; although it will help if the reader is able to bear in mind throughout what follows these and other philosophical antecedents of the inexpressibility thesis, not least because they help one to understand the general nature of the metaphysical impulses which have repeatedly led philosophers to advance such a thesis in its various historical forms and variants.

[2] Moritz Schlick, 'Form and Content, an Introduction to Philosophical Thinking' in *Gesammelte Anfsätze*, 1926–1936, Gerold and Co., Wien, 1938.

[3] J. J. C. Smart, 'Sensations and Brain Processes', *Philosophical Review*, LXVIII (1959), 141–56; 'Colours', *Philosophy*, *XXXVI* (1961), 128–142.

[4] B. A. Farrell, 'Experience', *Mind*, *LIX* (1950), 170–98.

II

According to Smart and Farrell, the most fundamental level of discourse about experience is the level at which we state the facts, so far as they are known to us, about our own and other's ability to discriminate between particular types of presented stimuli. If we ask whether there is not some more fundamental level at which we can describe the phenomenal character of the experiences between which we discriminate, the reply must be that there is not. Experience talk boils down ultimately to discrimination talk. Let us call this 'the discrimination thesis'.

Smart's and Farrell's ground for holding the discrimination thesis differ somewhat. Smart's argument, if I understand him correctly, is that acceptance of the thesis must follow acceptance of the doctrine that meaning is 'use', and not 'a mental experience which evokes and is evoked by a word',[5] once we fully understand what is involved in the latter doctrine. It is evident, Smart thinks, that a blind man who had the opportunity to study how normally sighted people sorted samples identified by physical and chemical criteria, and how they applied colour words to the resulting sets of samples, would eventually come to *use* colour words exactly as the sighted sorters use them. That is, he would use 'orange', for example, to mean something like 'resembling anything which a normally sighted person would, under normal conditions of illumination, sort into the same compartment as oranges, fashionable Swedish iron casseroles, . . .', and so on. We can still say, perhaps, that the blind man does not 'know what colours are', but this only means that he cannot use himself as a 'normal percipient', or to put it bluntly cannot see, which is trivially true.

Will this do? The bald assertion that 'Meaning is use' no

[5] 'Colours', p. 141.

longer counts, it seems to me, as the expression of a philosophical insight of the first water, even when the word 'use' is prudently enclosed, as Smart encloses it, in inverted commas. Before anything can be made of such a claim one needs to have a plain, preferably non-metaphorical, account of what the speaker understands by 'use', and this Smart does not provide. When he says that the blind man's 'use' of colour words would be equivalent, in the context of his example, to the 'use' made of them by the normally sighted, what Smart seems to mean is that for any statement about colour made by the sighted, an analytically equivalent statement could be found which would be capable of being known from experience to be true by Smart's blind man. If *this* were true, then the discrimination thesis would follow from it as a necessary consequence, but why should we accept it as true? If we are to accept that for *every* statement about colour which the sighted observer can make, an analytically equivalent one capable of being independently asserted by the blind man can be found, then we cannot, presumably, confine ourselves to attributing a contingent deficiency of expressive power to the particular natural language in which it happens that the sighted observer must articulate his remarks about colour. What we shall have to claim is that there exists a necessary deficiency of expressive power which (being necessary) afflicts every possible natural language, and which makes it impossible for language (language *per se* that is) to penetrate, as it were, below the level of recording discriminations and failures to discriminate, to the level of phenomenal description; description, that is, of what Smart would call the *qualia* of experience. But this raises obvious difficulties. How can we possibly hope to demonstrate any *necessary* truth about any subject matter as manifestly empirical and contingent as 'language' or 'experience'?

It might be argued at this point that the reason why language is necessarily incapable of being used to describe the *qualia* of experience is that there are simply no such things: our experience possesses structure but no content. But this will not do, for to assert this amounts simply to reasserting Smart's claim about the analytical equivalence in principle of the discourse of the sighted and the blind, and this is the very claim for whose assertion we are trying to find grounds.

I cannot find in Smart's discussions any clearly stated reason for accepting this claim. Farrell, however, does offer quite a powerful argument in its favour, and one or two remarks of Smart's suggest that he too has this argument in the back of his mind.

Farrell sees clearly that what the inexpressibility theorist must defend is the *necessary* inexpressibility of content. 'When we say "We can't describe the experience of seeing a red patch" (in the raw feel[6] sense) the "can't" is logical.'[7] He argues that the reason why the experience of seeing a red patch cannot (logically) be described, is that such an experience is 'featureless'.

'I shall say that the experience of X which we are alleged to be leaving out [when we describe the totality of X's verbal and behavioural response to a given stimulus] is featureless ... The experience of X is featureless because there is nothing about it that X can discriminate. If he does discriminate something that appears to be a feature of the experience this something at once becomes, roughly, either a feature of the stimulus in the sort of way that the saturation of the red in a red shape is a feature of the red shape, or a feature of his own responses to the shape.'[8]

Why can no features of raw feels be discriminated? The answer is to be found in Farrell's definition of a raw feel. When a given observer, confronted by a given stimulus pattern, has made *all* the discriminations which he is capable of making with respect to is, and has marked each of these discriminations

[6] Farrell means by 'raw feel' the phenomenal character of an experience. The term is adapted from Tolman, *Purposive Behaviour in Animals and Men.*

[7] Op. cit., p. 18.

[8] Op. cit., p. 178.

by some appropriate piece of verbal or non-verbal behaviour, what, by definition, remains to be described, if *per impossibile* such description were possible, is the 'raw feel' of the objects of perception between which he has been discriminating. Farrell amusingly documents the anguish of psychologists over their inability to describe such 'bare' experiences, and thus to complete in an objective and impersonal way the psychological description of experience. Farrell's point, however, is that just because when we reach the point at which we encounter raw feels, *all* possible discriminations have, *ex hypothesi*, been made, it is senseless (logically absurd) to demand of the observer that he make *further* discriminations with respect to those raw feels, and thus senseless to demand any kind of description, scientific or otherwise, of them.[9] Thus, if the argument works, Farrell has established both the inexpressibility thesis and the discrimination thesis, while avoiding the support of any such suspiciously corroded staff as the verification principle or the use theory of meaning, by demonstrating that the inexpressibility of the content of experience is, in a quite simple way, a logical consequence of our concept of experience itself.

[9] Farrell's argument at this point has general affinities with Locke. For Locke, as for most later empiricists, to state the meaning of an expression is in effect to treat it as an analysandum to be replaced in discourse by some analysans. The linguistic nature of this operation is obscured in Locke by the fact that for him, analysans and analysandum are conceived as psychological entities: ideas. But, nonetheless, to explain the meaning of the name of a complex idea is in effect, for Locke, to replace the complex idea in question with some set of simple ideas which can be displayed as standing in clear and comprehensible relationships to one another. A simple idea, now, just is an idea which can be subjected to no further analysis of this kind. Hence such simples are ultimate in our conceptual scheme, in the sense that they correspond to the concepts in terms of which all explications of meaning must ultimately be framed. Simple ideas then, in a sense, make possible all communication between men—and yet, paradoxically, just because they are simple (i.e. insusceptible of analysis) their nature remains itself incommunicable. They can perhaps be *identified* (by pointing, by reference to the contexts in which they occur) but they cannot be *described*. The extreme oddity of this position has not, I think, been generally appreciated even today.

III

But does Farrell's argument work? What we must first notice about this elegant and persuasive argument, I think, is that it derives the inexpressibility thesis from two premises, one concerning the nature of experience and the other the nature of linguistic description, and that it will not yield a proof of the thesis unless *both* these premises are in fact true. The two premises in question may, I think, be stated as follows:

(i) Perceptual discrimination has empirically discoverable limits: any observer, in the process of making finer and finer discriminations between stimuli of a given sort must reach a point at which he is unable to discriminate between certain stimulus-occurrences, which he must therefore admit to be qualitatively identical, although not, of course, numerically identical, since to say that *two* stimuli are qualitatively identical is precisely to say that *the same* stimulus, qualitatively speaking, can recur. (We shall say that when an observer is acquainted with such a stimulus occurrence he is acquainted with an *instance* of an *indiscriminable recurrent*)

(ii) When an observer marks a perceptual discrimination *behaviourally*, by responding differentially, say by button-pressing, to discriminable stimuli, he is doing something which is not essentially or importantly different from marking such a discrimination *verbally*, by assigning to the discriminable stimuli different names or descriptive phrases.

(i) seems to me to be relatively unexceptionable;[10] (ii) to be false.

[10] Problems arise from the fact that for three closely similar colours, A, B, C, A may be discriminable from C although it cannot be discriminated from B nor B from C. Farrell could, however, do justice to this possibility by quite simple modifications to his thesis, so for the sake of simplicity I shall ignore it in what follows.

We can see this if we look more closely at the way in which (ii) is involved in Farrell's argument, and at some of the consequences which flow from it if it is taken strictly and literally.

What Farrell's argument certainly shows is that there must be indiscriminable recurrents. It only shows, however, that indiscriminable recurrents are necessarily indescribable *if* describing something essentially amounts to discriminating some feature of it. This will be true if, and only if, a name or descriptive phrase functions semantically (that is, functions in its role as an element of a natural language) as label, or tag, for a given determinate stimulus in the same way that a behavioural response such as button-pressing may do. If describing is a form of behavioural tagging of discriminations then, manifestly, when there are no more discriminations to be tagged, description must have an end. But if description in language cannot be understood simply as a variant of behavioural tagging then it remains possible that some sort of linguistic description of the qualitative character of instances of indiscriminable recurrents might be feasible, and, since Farrell's argument contains no machinery for excluding this possibility then, in that case, Farrell will have failed to *demonstrate* the logical indescribability of raw feels and instead will simply have reduced the issue to one turning upon a Humean challenge: '*Show* me how raw feels are to be described.' And this is a challenge which I think, despite the contrary weight of three hundred years of Cartesian and British Empiricist dogma, admits of an answer, although a rather complicated one.

IV

Is it, then, reasonable to suppose that description in a natural language is essentially a form of behavioural tagging of stimuli? Let us call a language conceived in such a way a *discrimination language*. For the purpose of setting up such a language we have to conceive of its correlative extra-linguistic world—that world with which the semantic rules of the language connect its lexemes[11]—as an array of stimuli between any two of which an observer who uses the language can either discriminate or not discriminate. The assignment of meanings to the lexemes of a discrimination language in terms of the contents of this extra-linguistic world proceeds as follows: if the observer cannot discriminate between two stimuli he tags them with the same lexeme; if he can discriminate between them he tags each with a different lexeme.

This specification gives us a language with an extremely simple and restricted structure of semantic rules,[12] and it may be objected that it is obvious that no natural language could possibly be so restricted in its semantic mechanisms. This, I think, is true. My reasons for nonetheless proceeding to discuss discrimination languages are first, that this, as we have seen, is the model of the semantics of a natural language that one gets if one takes absolutely rigorously and literally the account of describing which is implicit in Farrell's argument, which itself is, in one form or another, very widely accepted among philosophers as sound; and second, that it is important to get clear not only that this model is inadequate as a theoretical representation of the semantics of a natural language, but also why it is inadequate.

In a discrimination language a given lexeme is presumably in practice given a meaning by being associated with one or more instances of some indiscriminable recurrent. The utterance of a given lexeme L at T_1 in response to some total stimulus-

---

[11] I wish to use 'lexeme' as a term denoting indifferently the members of any class of entities postulated at any level of linguistic description at which semantic rules may be supposed to operate. In my usage it is thus neutral with respect to degree of structural complexity: lexemes, for example, need not be, though they may be, morphemes.

[12] For examples of languages with more complex systems of rules see my *Meaning and Structure*, 'Studies in Language,' ed. Noam Chomsky and Morris Halle, Harper and Row, New York, 1972; 'Category Mistakes and Rules of Language', *Mind*, 1965.

pattern S_1 thus has (as its *use*, as Smart would say) the function of directing a hearer's attention to some previous stimulus-pattern S_0 by reference to which, at T_0, L was, for both speaker and hearer, assigned a meaning. If we think of the utterance of L as constituting the utterance of what Quine has called a 'one-word sentence' then the sentence 'L' might be regarded as equivalent to (as asserting the same proposition as) some English sentence of the form:

(1) S_0 and S_1 are indiscriminable.

This account of the signification of L is open to the objection that (1) fails to specify *in respect of what type of feature* S_0 and S_1 must be indiscriminable, in order that their indiscriminability may justify the utterance of L. It can be replied, however, that a well-designed discrimination experiment evades this difficulty by its design. We can, for example, test discrimination by using a specially designed array of colour chips, each of which is so similar to its fellows in shape, size, texture of surface and so on, that *only* their hues can in practice be used to discriminate one chip from another. We can thus, it seems, by operating at the empirical limits of the ability to perform sensory discriminations, use these very limits to single out from the ordinary confusion of sensory experience the type of sensory feature which we wish the lexemes of our discrimination language to denote.

When we try to apply this model of the semantic rules governing the denotation of basic sensory terms to natural languages, we encounter the following series of objections. The first is the relatively trivial one that it is difficult to differentiate hue from subjective brightness without the use of verbal directions. We will, however, simply assume that this difficulty is not insuperable. Secondly, and more seriously, in the universe of experience in which the colour vocabularies of natural languages are learned and used, well-designed arrays of colour chips are extreme rarities. We shall assume that this objection, too, can be answered and that something of the sort often described by psychologists in some such conventional phrase as 'the patterning of stimuli and reinforcements by the linguistic community' fulfils the function of singling out types of sensory feature which is performed in a different way by the design of a discrimination experiment.

There is, however, a third objection which I think is fatal to the thesis that natural languages, or those parts of them which handle reference to immediate sensory experience, are discrimination languages in the sense so far defined. It is that the colour concepts made available by a discrimination language are radically different in type from those made available by an ordinary natural language such as English.

The point which I wish to make is not easy to explain, for reasons which will become clear in a moment, without introducing a technical term, and this I shall now do, stifling in the interests of clarity a reasonable distaste for neologism in philosophy. I want to speak of a particular hue, presented in a certain definite degree of saturation and tonality,[13] as a *colour presentation*. The cover of this book, on this terminology, exhibits a certain colour presentation. Different areas of the cover, assuming the cover to be homogeneously coloured and not yet dappled with what a structuralist philosopher of my acquaintance felicitously calls 'the stains of human use', exhibit the same colour presentation. The cover of the next book on the shelf, however, in all probability exhibits a quite different colour presentation. In other words, colour presentations comprise one species of indiscriminable recurrents.

A 'colour' in English, and so far as I know in all other natural languages which have received careful study, is a set or category of colour presentations. Thus 'red' in English is equally correctly applicable to a very large number of distinct colour presentations, including, for example, scarlets, crimsons, some

[13] The latter terms are standard in the description of colour, but in any case will be explained here at a later point.

deep pinks, some reddish purples, and so on. In everyday English we do some justice to this fact by speaking of 'shades': we say things like 'a rather bluish shade of purple' for example. But 'shade' is not equivalent in meaning to 'colour presentation' as we have defined it above. People very often use 'shade' to mean simply 'hue': so that the same 'shade' of red could be presented in different degrees of saturation and tonality to yield what, in our terminology, would be different colour presentations.

Further possibilities of confusion arise from the fact that, while 'a colour'—e.g. red—is in English a category of colour presentations, the expressions 'the colour of x' and 'the same colour as x' are normally used not to refer to colour *category* but to colour *presentation*. Thus when I speak of 'the colour of this book' I do not generally mean to refer to the English colour category (e.g. blue) into which the colour presentation exhibited by the cover falls: I mean to refer to the particular colour-presentation which the cover exhibits. And similarly it would be very odd to say of two very differently coloured red things (one scarlet, one crimson, for example) that they were 'the same colour', for to say that two things are 'the same colour' normally means that they exhibit the same colour presentation or closely similar colour presentations.

Since technical terms carry their own possibilities of confusion, there is very little that one can do with ordinary English except use it and hope for the best. I shall therefore use the word 'colour' throughout what follows as it is ordinarily used, trusting to the term 'colour presentation' to help us to evade the possibilities of confusion implicit in ordinary usage.

My point against the thesis that the colour vocabularies of natural languages are discrimination languages is, now, precisely that the colour terms in a discrimination language are names for colour presentations, whereas the colour terms in natural languages are names for categories of colour presentation.

This fact is closely connected with a feature of natural language which has been exhaustively emphasized over the past ten years by linguists interested in the construction of generative grammars;[14] namely, that our use of language exhibits *creativity* or *originality*. Linguists have primarily concerned themselves with syntactic originality: they have pointed out that a native speaker's ability to construct and interpret syntactic structures is creative in the sense of not being limited in its exercise to the set of structures which have figured expressly in past learning situations. Someone who knows English has acquired, as a result of a finite period of language learning, the ability to assign or deny syntactic structures to a potentially infinite number of putative English sentences.[15] But it seems clear that our ability to name colours is creative in a closely related sense. That is, I do not need to be expressly told that a particular colour presentation is one of the group of colour presentations called, in English, 'blue' in order to recognize it as blue, and this remains true even if I have never before come across that particular colour presentation—if for example it is the colour of a newly synthesized dyestuff. As I admiringly watch the new compound precipitating in the retort I may indeed need to be told its molecular formula or the process by which it is made, but I shall hardly need to be told that it is *blue*.

[14] But of which Wittgenstein was well aware at the time of writing the *Tractatus*. The same point was discussed in the Thirties by writers of the Vienna Circle, particularly, as we shall see, by Moritz Schlick.

[15] 'The central fact to which any significant linguistic theory must address itself is this: a mature speaker can produce a new sentence of his language on the appropriate occasion, and other speakers can understand it immediately, though it is equally new to them. Most of our linguistic experience, both as speakers and hearers, is with new sentences; once we have mastered a language, the class of sentences with which we can operate fluently is so vast that for all practical purposes (and, obviously, for all theoretical purposes) we may regard it as infinite. Normal mastery of a language involves not only the ability to understand immediately an indefinite number of entirely new sentences, but also the ability to identify deviant sentences and, on occasion, to impose an interpretation on them., Noam Chomsky, *Current Issues in Linguistic Theory*, Mouton & Co., The Hague, 1964, p. 7.

I may even say, for example, 'That is a shade of blue the like of which I have never in my life seen.'

To possess the concept *blue* (to know the meaning of the English colour term 'blue') is, then, to possess the capacity to apply the term 'blue' to colour presentations which I have in no sense been *taught* to regard as blue. It seems clear that the description of a discrimination language which we have before us contains no explanatory machinery which could render explicable the acquisition of such a capacity. The speaker of such a language who has been taught to associate a particular lexeme with anything identical in colour with some specifically designated colour sample will be *a fortiori* prevented by the rules of his language from applying that lexeme to anything which is *discriminable* in colour from the sample in question, however *similar* in colour to that sample it may be. He will possess, not a *colour* name, but a name for one particular colour presentation. And he will be unable to attach any name to a colour presentation, unless the colour presentation in question is indistinguishable from that exhibited by some colour sample with which he has been made acquainted during the process of being taught the language, and with which a lexeme has been expressly associated. It is important to see, too, that we cannot arrive at the sort of colour-vocabulary characteristic of natural languages by postulating a very long and detailed process of discrimination-language teaching, in which great numbers of discriminable colour presentations are associated with lexemes *en bloc*, many hues to one lexeme. The postulation of such a process can in principle explain any finite particular sequence of associations of single colour names with hues by some finite set of speakers of a natural language over a finite period of time; but it cannot explain the open-ended capacity to name unfamiliar hues which is acquired in learning to speak a natural language. Moreover the postulation of such a process offers no explanation of the assignment of compound colour names to unfamiliar hues: for example 'a greenish blue', 'a deep

purpleish red'. We shall see later that the possibility of giving
such characterizations is an important feature of the colour
description system of natural languages.[16]

V

At this point it is worth pausing, however, to show that a
certain alternative account which might seen *prima-facie* rather
attractive will not do. It might seem that what is wrong with a
discrimination language is simply that it makes the location of
nameables depend upon whether or not successive colour presentations can be barely *discriminated*. Perhaps a more adequate model could be based upon the noticing of *similarities*
between colour presentations, since, after all, it seems not
unreasonable to suppose that what links colour presentations
together into the sets denoted by English colour terms are the
relationships of resemblance which subsist between them. It
might seem quite easy to restate the inexpressibility thesis in
terms of this model. Colour words, we might argue, refer to
patterns of similarities between colour presentations. A pattern
of similarities is an array of formal relationships of a certain
sort, and it seems logically possible, for example, that two sets
of colour presentations possessing no common member might
nevertheless each exhibit internally identical sets of similarity

---

[16] The *ad hoc* character—the generative infertility—of discrimination
languages perhaps explains why natural languages use other mechanisms
of colour reference. A generative system affords maximum communicative
power in return for minimal complication in the system of rules which
must be assimilated by the learner. In an *ad hoc* colour language based
upon inability to discriminate as its fundamental notion, the occasion to
use a colour word would rarely recur. Block association (many-one
association) would to some extent overcome this, but would still leave the
learner open to the possibility that some new hue (a new dyestuff e.g.)
might be unnameable, and would, in any case, be intrinsically much more
complicated than, for example, the structure of rules presented in Part 2 of
the present volume.

relationships amongst their respective members; so that in such a case the difference in content between the two sets would be in principle inexpressible in language.

This move, however, exposes the inexpressibility theorist to a further set of difficulties, which a more straightforward account, in terms of discrimination rather than similarity, avoids. We can best approach these by way of some further reflections on naming.

Naming, as we have seen, can be regarded as a device for making temporal cross-references between stimuli, and this is how the inexpressibility theorist does regard it. To attach a lexeme to a given total stimulus pattern is implicitly to assert (indeed, if we are prepared, like Quine, to countenance one-word indicative sentences, we can regard it as explicitly asserting) that that total stimulus pattern is in some sense *the same as* any other total stimulus pattern to which the same lexeme could be correctly attached. The trouble is, in what sense? Trivially, the answer to this question must be 'the same for the purpose of attaching this lexeme'; but what makes two stimulus patterns apt for the attachment of the same lexeme to each? There seem to me to be two possibilities. On the one hand, this question may be answered by the natural articulations of the given-in-experience, so that once we attach a lexeme at T_0 to a particular component of our experience *the natural articulations of things in our experience which define things of that sort as distinct components of our experience* themselves suffice to determine at what points in time $T_1, T_2, \ldots, T_n$ we are to reattach the lexeme to the shifting fabric of our experience. In this event we shall be able to speak of our experience as containing, or consisting of, *natural nameables*. The other alternative is that we ourselves, through the stipulation of rules or criteria of some sort, do some of the work of determining what consequences for our future lexeme-attaching behaviour at T_1, $T_2, \ldots, T_n$ are implicit in our attachment of a given lexeme at T_0 and thus, *per contra*, of course, of determining *what type of*

entity it was to which we attached the original lexeme at T_o.
To take this latter view is, I shall say, to hold that the lexemes
to which it applies designate *constructed nameables*.

Talk of 'natural nameables' perhaps makes it sound as
though I want to claim that naming might be thought of somehow as a 'natural' process, without any element of linguistic
convention; perhaps as something human beings do as a mere
causal consequence of the way in which they perceive the world.
This is not at all what I have in mind. Even if I can perceptually
discriminate something as a clearly defined feature of my en-
vironment prior to my acquisition of any linguistic capacities,
the mere act of pointing to that thing and uttering some lexeme
carries in itself no implication whatsoever for any future act of
pointing and lexeme-uttering. We can only extract such implications from the act in question if we suppose it to be carried out
by some person, or persons, who have adopted some such
linguistic rule as the following:

(2) Attach lexeme l to any object o_n of type T which is indistinguishable from (similar in respects $a, b, c \ldots$ to) the object,
o_1, of base attachment of l.

It is important to see that (2) is a *rule*, and that without it there
would be no (linguistic) procedure of lexeme 'attachment' at all.
We cannot reduce the conventional element in language to
nothing. On the other hand we can certainly imagine it, at
least, progressively reduced, and the notion of a language all
of whose basic lexemes denote natural nameables can be thought
of as the theoretical limit of this process of making more
parsimonious the system of rules which define constructed
nameables. The furthest we can go in this direction is, perhaps,
a language in which the fundamental rules governing the attachment and reattachment of lexemes have the general form of
(2), but in which the crucial expressions, 'object of type T',
'indistinguishable from', 'similar to in respects $a, b, c, \ldots$'

which occur in (2) are defined in terms of the criteria employed by the perceptual mechanisms which enable us to discriminate things of the type being named as distinct elements in our perceptual field. The reattachment of lexemes would thus depend only minimally upon anything describable as 'linguistic convention', and maximally upon those features of our experience which enable us to divide experience into distinct separable elements prior to, and quite independently of, any linguistic capacities which we may be imagined to acquire later on. The referents of the basic terms of such a language would thus in effect be defined as distinct objects of reference (nameables) independently of linguistic convention, and it is such objects of reference that I shall refer to as 'natural nameables' in what follows.

The referents of the terms in a discrimination language are natural nameables in this sense. That is, once we have defined a naming procedure by stipulating some such rule as (2), our experimental design—the use of standard colour chips and so forth—really does single out a class of natural nameables (i.e. colour presentations, considered as indiscriminable recurrents) which are simply given in experience. That is, we do not, as we have seen, given the design of our experimental situation, face the question (a) 'What constitutes a *hue*?' or (b) 'What entitles us to say that two objects are *of the same hue*?' For a hue is simply a member of that class of properties by reference to which alone our special colour chips can be told apart, while two hues are the same when, and only when, no subject can tell apart the chips which exhibit them. Given our experimental arrangements, that is, which define a certain limited field of experience, hues by their nature define themselves with respect to that field both as a type of property and as individual properties of that type.

The notion of a constructed nameable can best be understood by contrast with that of a natural nameable. The objects of reference corresponding to the terms of a natural language are constructed nameables just in case the terms 'object', indistinguishable from', 'similar in respects a, b, c, . . .', which occur in (2) are defined not merely by reference to the conditions of our pre-linguistic perceptual sensibility but also in part by reference to further linguistic conventions; that is, conventions going beyond (2) itself.

VI

If the referents of colour terms in a natural language can be construed as natural nameables, then it follows that the inexpressibility thesis is correct. For if the referents of colour terms are natural nameables, then what counts as a colour, and what colour presentations fall into the group of presentations to which I later learn to ascribe a particular colour name (for example 'red') are questions fully determined by the conditions of my pre-linguistic perceptual sensibility. In other words, the fabric of my experience, prior to the point at which I begin to learn language, is already divided into objects of various types (perceptual modalities, particular colours, and so on) between which I can discriminate. It now looks as though Farrell's account of language is quite correct. Language merely supplies conventional markers for these pre-existing perceptual discriminations by setting up a system of differential verbal responses, the utterance of which depends by convention upon the discriminability or indiscriminability of successive stimuli. And as we saw earlier, the inexpressibility thesis follows immediately from this account of the nature of language.

On the other hand, if the referents of the terms in our ordinary colour vocabulary are constructed nameables, then the inexpressibility thesis cannot be demonstrated in this short and satisfying way. It may still of course be demonstrable in other ways, but in order to arrive at a demonstration we should have to examine the additional rules (additional to rules of the same type as (2), that is) by means of which language resolves the questions about the composition and limits of classes which rules of type (2) leave open, but which must be settled if we are to explain how a given speaker of a natural language applies terms within roughly the same limits of application as those observed by other speakers of the same language. It might turn out that a thorough examination of these linguistic mechanisms would leave us still in a position to formulate some version of the inexpressibility thesis. But then again, it might not.

So far our argument has run as follows. Farrell's argument presupposes a view of languages according to which the basic colour terms in our language designate natural nameables. This is not implausible if we can suppose that the basic colour terms in our language designate particular colour presentations. For a colour presentation might seem to have a rather good claim to the status of a natural nameable. The necessary criterion of lexeme reattachment in the case of determinate colour terms is provided by our actual incapacity to distinguish between the objects simply by appeal to their colour when both exhibit the same colour presentation. The determinable 'colour', as we have seen, gives us a little more trouble. We have to discover a criterion for recognizing something as a colour. As we remarked earlier this can be done by using a special set of objects (standard colour chips) so constituted that in practice colour is the only criterion by reference to which one such object can be distinguished from another. And although it seems grossly improbable at first sight that the actual teaching of colour language is carried out in conjunction either with such sets of objects or with natural analogues of them, perhaps ingenuity might mitigate this initial implausibility.

The trouble with this, however, is that, however plausible the claim that colour presentations are natural nameables, it is demonstrably false that the basic colour terms in our language designate colour presentations. They designate colours, and colours are classes of colour presentations.

Different speakers of the same language assign the same colour term to (with minor variations) the same class of colour presentations, and the question confronting us now is: what accounts for this capacity? What are the criteria which the speaker uses to assign a given colour presentation to a given colour category (e.g. 'red') and what are his criteria for determining the limits of application of the term 'colour'? (How, in other words, does he answer, for particular colour terms and for the determinable 'colour', the questions presupposed by rules of type (2)?).

The suggestion that lies before us is that a sufficient answer to these questions is supplied by the natural (i.e. pre-linguistically discriminable) resemblances subsisting between colour presentations. A colour is, on this view, simply a class of natural resemblances, and the term 'colour', used as the name of a determinable universal, stands for the class of all such classes.

The trouble with this suggestion, I think, is that resemblance can serve as a principle upon which to connect things with one another but not as a principle upon which to separate things from one another. But it is the latter function which it is being called upon to serve here. We are told that a colour is a certain class of resemblances. Which class? Classes of resemblances are by their nature indefinitely extensible. Let us suppose that I exhibit two red colour presentations, r_1, r_2, and propose as a criterion for determining the limits of application for the term 'red' some such rule as the following:

(3) (i) Any colour presentation is a member of the class of red things if it resembles red colour presentations to the degree that red colour presentations resemble each other.
(ii) r_1 and r_2 are red colour presentations.

It is evident, I think, that this rule will entitle us to add more and more colour presentations to the category 'red' in serial order, but gives us no criterion whatsoever for refusing to admit a colour presentation to the category. The process of adding colour presentations to the category 'red' will thus go on until the colour universe has been exhausted. And it is not at all obvious how any criterion for stopping this process at a certain point can be extracted from the bare notion of resemblance. The notion of a 'class' of resemblances thus stands as much in need of explication as the notion of a class of colour presentations.

Similar problems arise with 'colour' construed as the name of a determinable universal. If we cannot define a colour as a class of resemblances, we cannot define 'colour' as the class of all such classes. And equally clearly if, choosing several diversely coloured objects, we attempt to indicate the scope of application of the term 'colour' by stipulating that any object is coloured which resembles these in just the degree and respects in which they resemble each other, we shall not succeed in distinguishing the application of 'colour' from that of 'brightness', or 'surface', or for that matter, from any other feature, quite unrelated to colour, in which an arbitrarily chosen set of paradigm objects may resemble one another (this latter possibility becomes stronger the larger the set of paradigms we use).

It might perhaps be thought that we could evade these difficulties by specifying that the crucial class of similarities is precisely that class, attention to which would lead a subject to arrange colour samples exactly as a competent speaker of English does when he arranges such samples under the headings 'red', 'green', 'yellow' etc.

But this is a wholly unenlightening move. What we wish to know is, precisely, what the competent speaker of English does when he assigns colour names, and that involves knowing how he singles out (by reference to what criteria he singles out) certain classes of colour presentations from amongst the indefinite number of possible groupings and regroupings into which the experiential material to which he has access in perception might equally well be ordered. Our problem is not, of course, the psychological one of whether, or how, the subject *sees colours*. The first of these questions we can answer by appeal to discrimination tests, the second would take us into the anatomy and physiology of vision. Our question concerns the nature of what is learned by someone who learns to assign the members of a certain class of words to certain features of his experience in ways which always turn out, barring colour blindness or disagreements about very fine distinctions of hue, to coincide with the assignments made by other native speakers. And this, as we shall argue in a moment, is a question not about his psychology but about the rule-structure of his language.

Let us sum up this preliminary stage of the discussion. It seems clear that while colour presentations can, up to a point at least, be regarded as natural nameables, colours (that is to say the entities denoted by the colour terms of ordinary English) cannot. A *colour* is not a self-individuating element of our experience,[17] whose very nature settles out of hand all questions about the present and future attachment of colour names. And hence, since natural languages with colour vocabularies obviously exist, so that such questions must clearly be settled by some means, we must look elsewhere to discover what it is that settles them. And the only alternative answer seems to be that they are settled by some stipulated rule or convention to which all speakers of the language adhere: that, in short, colours are constructed nameables.

There is at stake here a point of general philosophical importance. Philosophers are accustomed to the idea that experience presents us—or seems to present us—with various types of objects: material things such as tables or clouds;

[17] I am not, of course, saying that *colour* is unreal or in any way 'constructed' by us, and still less—what would surely be transparently absurd—that our experience of colour is a sort of figment of our linguistic conventions. *Colour*—what we perceive—is the total set of colour presentations. *A* colour (red, green, for example) is the denotatum of a colour term in a particular language.

sounds; pains; pangs and tingles; the sort of things I have described as colour presentations; perhaps even (although few philosophers would care to go this far) persons, and so on. There is a good deal of discussion about which of these sorts of object must be treated as primitive and fundamental and which can be treated as 'constructions' in some logical or transcendental sense of that term. But I think most philosophers take it for granted that there is no difference at all between speaking of 'objects' of experience in this sense and speaking of 'objects' of reference of terms in a language. They assume, that is, that the articulations, or structures, which divide experience into distinct classes of perceptual object, and individuate objects within these classes, are identical with the articulations which divide experience for the purpose of linguistic reference. This conflation is no doubt made easier by the undiminished popularity of associative/ostensive theories of meaning. If words acquire meaning merely by being ostensively associated with features of experience, then the individuation of the features in question must be prior to, and independent of, language. If we are correct, however, matters may be more complicated than this. We have begun to discover grounds for thinking that objects of experience and objects of reference may be radically different types of entity. On this view, objects of reference are linguistic entities, in the sense that their individuation is accomplished not merely by the nature of our prelinguistic perceptual sensibility (however the latter may be described) but through the addition to this, as it were, conceptual substratum, of some system of linguistic rules. We shall make use of this suggestion in what follows.

VII

Someone might object that our discussion so far has been essentially concerned with *what happens when a child learns his native language*, and that this is not a philosophical problem, but a problem for empirical psychology.

In fact we are not at all concerned with empirical questions about language learning, and neither, for that matter, are Smart and Farrell. When the inexpressibility theorist puts forward, explicitly or by implication, a thesis about the nature of meaning and reference in language, we should not, unless we merely wish to score a trivial debating point at his expense, take him to be putting forward a *causal* thesis. He should not for example, that is, be taken to be claiming that *as a matter of fact* the repeated utterance by a teacher of a certain lexeme in circumstances in which a learner is attending to a given sample discriminable only in hue from other samples in whose presence another lexeme or no lexeme is uttered by the teacher (or the process described by any other rigmarole which the reader may care to insert here) is *causally* necessary and/or *causally* sufficient for the successful learning of the meaning of lexemes of the type in question. We ought not, in charity, to put such a construction on the inexpressibility theorist's claim because (i) no evidence for any such *factual* claim is ever presented and it is in fact rather hard to see how any such evidence could be acquired, and (ii) even if such evidence were to be adduced the claim itself would be theoretically quite trivial and unenlightening. It is possible that eating mango pips might turn out to be causally sufficient and/or necessary to confer *ex nihilo* upon unsuspecting British diners a complete grasp of the Gujarati language. Such a discovery would in itself be of no theoretical interest whatsoever for the student of language, since it would throw no light upon the one question which, in these or any other circumstances, he would wish to have answered: what is it that the remarkable pips, in conferring a grasp of Gujarati, confer?

We can in fact distinguish two quite different questions about 'the nature of language'. viz.

Q_1 What is acquired in acquiring the ability to use and understand a natural language *ab initio*?

Q_2 What are the causal mechanisms, or the causally necessary and/or causally sufficient conditions of the initial learning of a natural language?

Most philosophical 'theories of meaning' have attempted to answer both questions simultaneously without clearly distinguishing between them: this accounts both for the peculiar unsatisfactoriness of discussion on the topic and for its resistance to 'therapeutic' dissolution. For obvious reasons of the sort given above, Q_2 does not seem to me to be a question which can be fruitfully tackled by philosophers, or for that matter by psychologists if they approach Q_2 without having in mind any glimmering of an answer to Q_1. Q_1 on the other hand is an intelligible and perhaps answerable question, and I think we must construe the inexpressibility theorist's thesis, so far as it is not merely a foredoomed attempt to do empirical psychology by the light of neither theory nor experiment, as an attempt to answer Q_1.

But once we state Q_1 clearly, certain quite strict criteria of adequacy for proposed answers to it make themselves apparent, including at least the following one.

(CA_1) An account of what is learned in learning a first language, if it is to possess any explanatory force, must avoid using as an unanalysed primitive notion, any concept c, if the application of c can only be explained within the context of the theory by being exemplified through the presentation of sample expressions in some natural language. Such an account may, however, make use of such concepts to locate the linguistic phenomena which it proposes to explain.

(CA_1) is perhaps not immediately intelligible as it stands. My intentions in formulating it is this. The ability to use a language, like the ability to ride a bicycle, is not entirely perspicuous to the possessor. We can know what *balancing* is and still not know what exactly we do when we balance, and we can know what a *general name* is and still be unsure about what it is that we do in applying general names (a state of ignorance to which much of the development of the theory of universals bears witness). We normally explain notions like that of a general name (or a sentence, or an article, or a definite description) by reference to examples of word-use or sentence construction. It is obviously essential that we should use such concepts in any theory in which we wish to talk about general terms, sentences, and so on, since otherwise we should have no means of locating or referring to the linguistic phenomena which interest us. But if a theory which sets out to explain what is learned in learning to use a general term can evade certain difficulties or lacunae in the explanation which it offers *only* by assuming the truth of some proposition which uses the everyday intuitively based concept of a general term, then we shall have illicitly assumed that the capacity to use general terms is perspicuous to its possessor in the very way in which, if there is anything in the matter for us to theorise about in the first place, it is not. And hence our theory will be trivial because circular, having committed a sort of *petitio principii*. The rationale of CA_1 is, then, the avoidance of this sort of circularity.

When I say, now, that the theoretical specification of a strict discrimination language singles out a class of natural nameables, what I mean is that it is free from this sort of circularity, at least as far as the questions (a) and (b) are concerned. What constitutes a *colour*, and what it is for two samples to be *of the same colour* can be explained by reference to the design of the matching experiment, and to an operationally defined primitive capacity of any subject to match colour samples of the specified sort in ways which conform to the practice of other subjects, without using any concept which we should need to explain by reference to linguistic examples: without using, for example, the concept of *being able to use the word 'hue'*

But if we turn to the weaker and more liberal formulation of the inexpressibility theorist's case in terms of the notion of resemblance between, we find that it does not avoid the sort of circularity which (CA_1) prohibits. The limits of classes of colour presentations cannot be specified by appeal to the bare notion of resemblance, and the theorist is reduced to specifying the resemblances he has in mind merely as those by attention to which one speaker is enabled to apply colour terms in ways which match their application by other speakers.

I am not suggesting, of course, that there is any difficulty in understanding how someone recognizes an object to be the same or similar in hue to one which he has seen elsewhere; not, of course, because there are not difficulties (of a psychological and physiological character) involved in understanding such phenomena of memory and recognition, but because the phenomena in question are entirely irrelevant to our present inquiry. We are concerned, not with how a man recognizes objects as similar or identical in hue to one another, but with how he manages systematically to apply colour terms in such a way as to match the usage of other native speakers of his language.

PART 2

Schlick on Form and Content:
A Tractarian Excursion

2. Schlick on Form and Content: A Tractarian Excursion

I

It is not by any means obviously silly to attempt to identify colours with systems of natural resemblances. Such a theory springs from a sensible enough thought: that what enables us to identify colours as a distinct and clearly delineated category of qualities, distinct from, say, degrees of brightness or conditions of surface texture, is that a large variety of relationships subsist between different colour presentations, in virtue of which all colour presentations hang together in a single relational system when considered as exemplars of hues, in a different relational system when considered as exemplars of relative degrees of brightness, in a third when considered as exemplars of relative degrees of saturation, and so on.

The interest of Moritz Schlick's lectures on *Form and Content*[1] lies partly in the fact that Schlick takes this thought seriously. Instead of taking the notion of a 'set' or 'system' of natural resemblances for granted, he makes a serious effort to get clear about what sorts of relationship actually do subsist between colour presentations.

Let us ... examine the verbal expressions of our ordinary language, i.e. the sentences and the words by which I give a description of our particular green colour. We easily discover an essential feature which they all have in common: they

[1] Loc. cit.

assign 'green' a certain place within a comprehensive system of shades, they speak of it as belonging to a certain order of colours. They assert, for instance, that it is a bright green, or a rich green, or a bluish green, that it is similar to this, less similar to that, equally dark as that, and so on; in other words, they try to describe the green by comparing it to other colours. Evidently it belongs to the intrinsic nature of our green that it occupies a definite position in a range of colours and in a scale of brightness, and this position is determined by relations of similarity and dissimilarity to the other elements (shades) of the whole system.

These relations which hold between the elements of the system of colours are, obviously, internal relations, for it is customary to call a relation internal if it relates two (or more) terms in such a way that the terms cannot possibly exist without the relation existing between them—in other words, if the relation is necessarily implied by the very nature of the terms. Thus, all relations between numbers are internal: it is in the nature of six and twelve that the one is half the other, and it would be nonsense to suppose that instances might be found in which twelve would not be twice as much as six. Similarly, it is not an accidental property of green to range between yellow and blue, but it is essential to green to be related to yellow and blue in this particular way, and a colour which was not so related to them could not possibly be called 'green' unless we decide to give to this word an entirely new meaning. In this way every quality (for instance, the qualities of sensation; sound, smell, heat, etc., as well as colour) is interconnected with all others by internal relations which determine its place in the system of qualities. It is nothing but this circumstance which I mean to indicate by saying that the quality [the particular shade of green, i.e.] has a certain logical structure.[2]

[2] Schlick, op cit., pp. 161–2. Schlick was not, of course, the first to notice that internal relationships obtain between simple sensory qualities, although

To describe these relationships as *logical* might seem an odd misuse of the word 'logic': The explanation is that Schlick's thought in these lectures is profoundly influenced, as we shall see, by Wittgenstein's *Tractatus Logico-Philosophicus*. 'Logical structure' for Schlick has associations with the Tractarian notion of 'logical form'. The theory of meaning which Schlick puts forward in the lectures, and on which his version of the inexpressibility thesis is based, has close affinities with the so-called 'Picture Theory of Meaning' in the *Tractatus*. Schlick's version, however, differs from Wittgenstein's in that Schlick makes a resolute attempt to convert what in Wittgenstein is an almost wholly abstract discussion of the general nature of signification into an account of the manner in which language is connected with experience.

Schlick begins by anticipating a number of points about the peculiar character of natural languages which have recently been made familiar, at least among linguistics, by the work of Noam Chomsky. Like Chomsky he distinguishes beween a language and a repertory of signals,[3] and says that the essential

---

he was, perhaps, first to notice or to think it important that they form systems, or matrices, within which individual qualities *intrinsically* possess definite locations. Hume at times comes close to seeing this (see, for example, the footnote to the chapter on 'Innate Ideas', *Treatise*, I. 1. vii).

[3] 'Expression is entirely different from mere Representation, it is much more and cannot be derived from it. Genuine speech is something entirely new as compared with the simple repetition of signs whose meanings have been learned by heart ...

... If language were nothing but a system of signs with fixed significations it would never be capable of communicating new facts. If its function consisted solely in representing thoughts or facts by means of symbols it could represent only such thoughts or facts to which a sign had been attached; a new fact would be one to which no symbol had been assigned, it would therefore be impossible to communicate it ... This state of affairs is made very clear by what is often called the 'language' of certain animals such as bees and ants ... The signals of bees and ants represent or indicate certain occurrences, they do not express them. They are restricted to these particular states of affairs, and cannot represent anything else. The essential characteristic of languages, on the other hand, is its capability of expressing

feature of the former is that it can communicate new facts by allowing the construction (as distinct from the express stipulation) of new signs which express those facts; whereas the latter is merely a list of associative symbols with no combinatory potential, and can hence express only the fixed range of facts with which the individual members of the list have been associatively linked. Furthermore Schlick, like Chomsky, locates the distinguishing line between animal and human 'language' in the transition from repertory 'language' to languages with combinatory or generative potential. Schlick introduces, to express this distinction, the contrasting terms 'representation' and 'expression'. A system of signs 'represents' states of affairs in the world simply by associating a sign with each state of affairs. Such a language can only represent the states of affairs with which the individual signs composing it have been linked: it cannot represent new states of affairs. A language 'expresses' states of affairs, on the other hand, if it allows the possibility of constructing, from the simple signs of the language, complex expressions which correspond to new facts.

Schlick's discussion here exactly parallels a (far more condensed and cryptic passage of the *Tractatus:*

4.02   ... we understand the sense of a propositional sign without its having been explained to us ...

4.024   To understand a proposition means to know what is the case if it is true.

(One can understand it, therefore, without knowing whether it is true.)

facts, and this involves the capability of expressing new facts, or indeed any facts. A schoolboy opens his copy of Xenophon's Anabasis, and by reading the first sentence of the book he learns the fact, which (let us assume) is entirely new to him, that King Darius had two sons. He knows what particular fact is expressed by that particular sentence, although he never came across that sentence before and certainly did not know the fact before. He therefore cannot have learned that the one corresponds to the other.'—*Form and Content*, loc. cit., pp. 155–6.

It is understood by anyone who understands its constituents.

4.025 When translating one language into another, we do not proceed by translating each *proposition* of the one into a *proposition* of the other, but merely by translating the constituents of propositions.

(And the dictionary translates not only substantives, but also verbs, adjectives, and conjunctions etc., and it treats them all in the same way.)

4.026 The meanings of simple signs (words) must be explained to us if we are to understand them.

With propositions, however, we make ourselves understood.

4.027 It belongs to the essence of a proposition that it should be able to communicate a new sense to us.

4.03 A proposition must use old expressions to communicate a new sense.

Both Schlick and Wittgenstein see the distinction beween names (or sequences of names) and propositions as consisting in the fact that a proposition can express 'a new sense'. Both hold that the central problem of the theory of meaning is to explain how this is possible.

The capacity of language to express new senses, Schlick goes on to argue, clearly depends upon the possibility of re-ordering the elements of compound signs to form new compound signs. Thus, for example, if we understand the meaning of:

(1) The ring is lying on the book

then, if we rearrange the parts of (1) to form

(2) The book is lying on the ring

'we understand the meaning of the second proposition immediately, without explanation'.[4]

4 Op. cit., p. 157.

The fact that language allows this kind of re-ordering seems, to Schlick, to entail two general propositions about the nature of language.

The first is that what makes a row of words into a proposition —what makes it express a fact—must be a correspondence in structure between the expressive fact (the written or spoken sentence) and the fact which it expresses.[5] For structure is the only thing that differentiates (1) and (2); hence it is by reference to the structure of the two sentences, and to that alone, that we are able to identify the very different states of affairs which the two sentences express.

The astute reader will notice that in the last half-page or so we, and Schlick, have passed from speaking of propositions expressing *senses* to speaking of them as expressing *facts*, and also that we have begun to use 'proposition' and 'sentence' as if they were synonymous. The explanation of both transitions is the same. Once we have been persuaded that difference in syntactic structure alone can produce two sentences expressing quite different propositions it becomes easy to regard structure alone as the determinant of propositional content in sentences. If we ask how this can be, the obvious answer which suggests itself is that the structure of the sentence somehow locates a corresponding structure 'in the world' and that this structure identifies what it is that the statement asserts to be the case. It is now very tempting to reify the second structure—the one 'in the world'—and to speak of such structures as 'facts' or 'states of affairs'. It now also becomes relatively indifferent whether we speak of the vehicle of assertion as a sentence or as a proposition. It is the structure of the sentence, and the correspondence of that structure with the structure of some possible state of affairs, which makes it express a proposition; but by the

[5] 'One and the same fact may be expressed in a thousand different languages, and the thousand different propositions will all have the same structure, and the fact which they all express will have the same structure, too, for it is just for this reason that all those propositions express just this particular fact', op cit., p. 158.

same token if the sentence did not express a proposition it would not be a sentence but merely a sequence of words.

This account of the difference between words and sentences, however, confronts us with a problem, which in turn will lead to the second of the general propositions mentioned above, and, incidentally, back to Schlick's reflections on the internal relations of colours. What enables me to identify, merely by inspecting the structure of a new sentence, the state of affairs (fact) which that sentence expresses? It cannot, clearly, be a conventional association between that structure and the state of affairs which it expresses, for *ex hypothesi* no such association has been set up (the sentence would not be 'new' in the required sense if it had). And equally, I cannot discover what fact it is that the sentence expresses by carrying out any empirical test or verification procedure. Empirical tests may indeed establish the truth of a sentence once I know what it asserts, but until I know what it asserts (what fact it expresses) the sentence is merely a string of words which simply has no *point d'appui* in the extra-linguistic world. Plainly, part of the answer must be that the words which make up the sentence locate at least the features of the world which enter into the fact which the sentence expresses. Sentences thus express, in effect, modes of relationship of the features of the world denoted by the names which enter into their composition. But from this it follows that in order to construct new sentences we must know in advance the possible modes of relationship into which the features in question can enter. Hence the basic objects of reference with which names are correlated must stand to one another in an *a priori* order of possibilities of relationship.

The study of the ways in which words can be combined or recombined to form significant sentences is *grammar*: or, if the naked term 'grammar' seems to carry too strong a suggestion that the possibilities of recombination are determined by mere linguistic convention, *logical grammar*. The arguments we have been outlining thus lead to the view that grammar (the order of possibilities of significant recombination of words) is a direct reflection of the structure of facts: that is to say, of the natural order of possibilities of combination of objects (the things with which basic names are correlated) in states of affairs.

This position, while very much simplified, approximates in outline to the theory of meaning which Wittgenstein puts forward in the *Tractatus*. 'Logical space'[6] in Tractarian terms is the order of possibilities of relationship (in *sachverhalten*) between the objects of reference (*dingen*)[7] of basic names in a language. The fundamental relationship linking language with the world holds, not between names and their referents, but between a sentence as a *structured* sequence of signs (a sequence of signs exhibiting, in Wittgenstein's terms, a *logical form*[8] and some *group* of things in the world standing in some possible set of relationships to one another, so that the relationships holding between the members of the group (the structure of the fact, or better, state of affairs) is mirrored by the structure (the logical form) of the sentence. This, I think, is what Wittgenstein means by the second sentence of the *Tractatus:* 'The world is the totality of facts, not of things.'[9] The logical priority of 'facts' as against 'things' is guaranteed in the *Tractatus* by the fact that things cannot be conceived independently of their possibilities of relationship within states of affairs.

> If I know an object I also know all its possible occurrences in states of affairs
>
> (Every one of these possibilities must be part of the nature of the object)
>
> A new possibility cannot be discovered later (2.0123)

The relationship between an object and its possibilities of occurence in states of affairs is thus internal. It is important to see, however, that Wittgenstein is not saying that the relation-

[6] L. Wittgenstein, *Tractatus Logico-Philosophicus*, tr. D. F. Pears and B. F. McGuinness, Routledge and Kegan Paul, 1961.
[7] Op. cit. 2.01.   [8] Op. cit. 3.14–3.142.   [9] Op. cit. 1.1.

ships which link objects into states of affairs are internal relationships for if this were so it would remove the possibility of asserting contingent propositions about states of affairs. The sort of things Wittgenstein has in mind when he says that possibilities of combination are intrinsic properties of object is further explained in 2.013–2.0141.

2.013   Each thing is, as it were, in a space of possible states of affairs. This space I can imagine empty, but I cannot imagine the thing without the space

2.0131 A spatial object must be situated in infinite space. (A spatial point is an argument-place). A speck in the visual field, though it need not be red, must have some colour: it is, so to speak surrounded by colour-space. Tones must have *some* pitch, objects of the sense of touch *some* degree of hardness, and so on.

2.014   Objects contain the possibility of all situations

2.0141 The possibility of its occurring in states of affairs is the form of an object.

The nature of objects is not further specified in concrete terms, and objects are never identified with any particular class of objects of experience.

The distinction between an order of relationships in the world which guarantees the possibility of the states of affairs expressed by sentences in a language, and the circumstances which establish the *truth* or *falsity* of a given sentence, leads directly to the celebrated—indeed notorious—Tractarian distinction between what can be *said*, or asserted, about the world, and what can only be *shown* by our use of language. If a sentence—or rather its structure, or logical form, expresses a given state of affairs, according to Wittgenstein, then what the sentence states is that that state of affairs obtains in the world, or 'is the case'. The sentence is true just in case the state of affairs *does* obtain (is 'the case'). The relationship of possibility of combination between *dingen* (basic objects of reference) which the sentence reflects in its own structure, is not, however, *asserted* by the sentence, but merely *shows* itself in the fact that we can seriously raise the question of the truth or falsity of the sentence. If, now, we try to construct a sentence which *asserts* this relationship between *dingen*—which says something like '*dingen* can be related in the following way, among others, viz, ——', we run into an obvious theoretical difficulty. We can only refer to *dingen* by naming them. We can only identify them for the purposes of naming them by reference to the relationships which can obtain between them. We can only refer to such a relationship by constructing a syntactic model of the relationship in question; that is, a sentence which mirrors the relationship in its syntactic structure. But now we have our original sentence, which shows but does not assert the relationship which guarantees its possibility (its 'making sense'); and not at all the sentence we wanted. In the end we can only gesture towards the relationships between *dingen* which constitute the fabric of initial possibilities on which in turn the possibility of assertion rests; or, what comes to the same thing, exhibit (show) their existence by the very sureness with which we construct and interpret new sentences in our language.

II

It is notorious that Wittgenstein never identifies *dingen* with any definite class of objects of experience, despite the fact that *dingen* are conceived as the referents of names in fully analysed sentences, and that fully analysed sentences must presumably stand in some relationship to what we actually experience. *Dingen*, in the *Tractatus*, remain in a certain sense purely theoretical objects: that is, they are postulated in order to satisfy certain theoretical requirements of the theory of meaning (that there should be 'definiteness of sense'; that we should know *a priori* and with certainty the possibilities of recombining sentence-elements to form new significant sentences) and they are specified no further than is absolutely necessary in order for them to satisfy these requirements.

Oddly enough, Schlick's discussion in *Form and Content*, profoundly Tractarian though it is, contains no theory of objects. The whole problem of how names refer, and what it is that they refer to, receives very little mention. Schlick does however, cleave firmly to the Tractarian distinction between, on the on hand, an order of external relationships between things in the world which constitute the 'structure' which contingent propositions 'express' (in Tractarian terms, 'mirror'); and on the other hand, an order of internal relationship which determine logical grammar, or the possibilities of combining names in discourse.

> It is clear that in speaking of colours or other 'qualities' we can refer to them only as external properties of something: we have to define a certain flavour as the sweetness of sugar, a certain colour as the green of a meadow . . .
> . . . it becomes evident that propositions express facts in the world by speaking of objects and their external properties and relations. And it would be a serious misunderstanding . . . if you believed that propositions could speak of logical structures or express them in the same sense in which we speak of objects and express facts. Strictly speaking none of our sentences about the green leaf expresses the internal structure of the green; nevertheless it is revealed by them in a certain way, or—to use Wittgenstein's term—it is shown forth by them. The structure of 'green' *shows itself in the various possibilities of using the word 'green', it is revealed by its grammar.* A language does not, of course, express its own grammar, but it shows itself in the use of language.

If the internal relationships which relate colour presentations determine 'the various possibilities of using the word green', it might reasonably seem to follow that Schlick identifies colour presentations—that is colour content, or *qualia*, with Wittgenstein's *dingen*. Nothing could be further from Schlick's mind. What Schlick wishes to show is not merely that content is inexpressible, but that there is no such thing as content; that the very word 'content' is without meaning.

There is no proposition about content, there cannot be any. In other words: it would be best not to use the word 'content' at all, there is no need for it, and my only excuse for using the word (even in the title of these lectures) is that this forbidden road seemed to me to be the easiest way of taking the reader to a point which will allow him to get a first view of the land before him. He will now be able to turn back and find the right road which will actually take him to the promised land. I shall continue to use the term 'content' now and then, but the reader will understand that a sentence in which this word occurs must not be regarded as a proposition about something called 'content' but as a sort of abbreviation of a more complicated sentence in which the word does not occur.[10]

This, in a way, is a tempting way out. Wittgenstein's account of *dingen* is metaphysical and obscure; it seems impossible to connect them with anything in our experience. What better than to transmogrify them into internally related contents and then somehow reductively analyse them out of existence?

There are, of course, severe difficulties about the introduction of colour contents to fill the theoretical role played in the *Tractatus* by *dingen*: that of accounting for the possibilities of combination exhibited by names in discourse. *Dingen*, like colour contents, are indeed internally related, but the internal relationships in question seem to be of radically different types.

[10] Op. cit., p. 176–7.

Dingen are internally characterized by their possibilities of combination in states of affairs. Colour contents are internally related into sequences of hue, or relative brightness or darkness, in virtue of their qualitative character. It is very difficult to see how *these* relationships could possibly govern the 'grammar' of a colour word as Schlick suggests, and Schlick does not elaborate or clarify his suggestion.

And yet Schlick has accepted so much of the argument that leads Wittgenstein in the *Tractatus* to postulate *dingen* that he can hardly do without them. His way out of this apparent impasse is to claim that the argument itself is a tissue of trivialities.

'In order to be able to describe the world we must be able to speak of all possible facts including those which do not exist at all, for language must be able to deny their existence. One might think that in saying this we are making rather bold *a priori* statements about the world. For are we not implying that all possible things or events in the world must conform to certain conditions, must possess a certain kind of order which will enable us to grasp them by means of our expressions? And would this not mean a metaphysical presupposition which could never be justified?

It is of the highest importance to see that in maintaining that facts must have a structure we are not making any presuppositions about the facts at all, we are saying only that facts are facts, which is, as will probably be admitted, saying nothing about them.[11]

All that Schlick has earlier said about the logical structure of colour is thus dismissed as vacuous or tautologous. The intrinsic implausibility of the claim is somewhat mitigated by Schlick's promise to show that all talk of content is a mere *façon de parler*, useful only in so far as it may help to carry the

[11] Op. cit. p. 158.

reader to a point from which he may clearly see the vacuity of such talk. Proposition 6.54 of the *Tractatus*[12] is clearly in the back of Schlick's mind.

But the resolute paradoxicality of 6.54 is foreign to Schlick's straightforward mind, and his words on pp. 176–7, which I quoted a few pages ago, suggest something more on the lines of a reductive analysis of sentences involving the notion of content. And this is, in the end, what Schlick offers. To understand the turns of his thought at this point we must remember that structure for him means not only the internal relationships of 'logical structure', but the external relationships which constitute facts. It is only the latter that propositions can express, so that *a fortiori* all propositions are contingent propositions.

So far as Schlick fills in, later on in the lectures, the claim that there can be no propositions about content, it would appear that he intends it to be construed as follows. A sentence is meaningless unless we can 'define the use' of the symbols it contains.[13] Defining a symbol involves exhibiting the rules according to which it is to be used, and 'These rules must be taught by actually applying them in definite situations, that is to say, the circumstances to which they fit must actually be shown ... And this can be done only by certain acts, as for instance gestures, by which our words and expressions are correlated to certain experiences.'[14] Now, to correlate a sentence with the world is to place it in just such a relationship with some fact that between it and the fact in question there exists that structural parallelism which Schlick regards as constitutive of the semantic function of the sentence. But to say this amounts precisely to saying that to give a meaning to a sentence is always to give it a meaning in terms of structure. 'A proposi-

---

[12] 'My propositions serve as elucidations in the following way: anyone who understands me eventually recognizes them as nonsensical, when he has used them—as steps—to climb up beyond them. (He must, so to speak, throw away the ladder after he has climbed up it).'

[13] Op. cit., p. 180.   [14] Op. cit., p. 180–1.

tion will be verified, the truth will be established if the structure is the same as the structure of the fact it tries to express.'[15] Hence no sentence can have as its truth conditions any state of 'content', and hence there can be no 'propositions about content'; and any sentences in ordinary language which apparently express propositions of this sort do so in appearance only and are in fact meaningless.

We have thus arrived at a new version of the inexpressibility thesis. But Schlick's argument seems to me to have serious defect. How can we place sentences in structural correlation with facts? How do we know what 'structure' in the world a given sentence picks out? A sentence, after all, is no more than a collocation of words. The obvious answer which springs to mind, I think, is that when we place the names in a sentence in correlation with things in the world, the external relations in which those things stand to one another can be represented in various ways by the external relations between the words in the sentence.

This is very much the direction Schlick takes. According to Schlick, a proposition is 'given a logical structure and a meaning . . . by assigning definite significations to its parts', and that, to see how this is done, 'we must imagine all the words of the sentence to be replaced by their definitions, the terms occurring in the definition must be replaced by sub-definitions and so on until we reach the boundary of ordinary verbal language when it ends in gestures or prescription to perform certain acts.'[16] In other words, a proposition acquires logical structure and meaning when we give, by means of deictic gestures, ostensive definitions of the words which it contains. Wittgenstein says very similar things in the *Tractatus*.

3.202 The simple signs employed in proposition are called names.

[15] Op. cit., p. 228.   [16] Op. cit., p. 228.

3.203 A name means an object. The object is its meaning.
('A' is the same sign as 'A')

3.21 The configuration of objects in a situation corresponds
to the configuration of simple signs in a propositional
sign

4.22 An elementary proposition consists of names. It is a
nexus, a concatenation of names.

Both these views suggest an account of language in which
the only *conventional* operation involved in setting up a language consists in placing names in correlation with objects. The
objects in question must be presumed to be natural nameables:
for they must be apprehended by us as distinct and clearly
individual objects prior to the inception of language if we are
to be able to carry out the association of name with object upon
which *ex hypothesi* language is founded. But—and this is what
I want chiefly to draw attention to—we must also suppose, on
this account of language, that the objects to which we attach
the basic names in our language are so constituted that, once
we have attached names to them, we can proceed to form these
names into sentences, which assert definite propositions, merely
by correlating the modes of arrangement of the linguistic signs
in each sentence with the external relationships holding between
some group of the objects in question. This amounts to the
view that *syntax*, in the linguistic sense, and the structure of our
experience are one and the same, since the structure of the world
can be made to determine the structure of sentences by the mere
act of associating names with nameables, and configurations of
names with configurations of nameables.

I shall call this theory the theory that *syntax* is *natural*. It
holds that the syntax of a language can be determined by
linguistic conventions which amount merely to associative
stipulations. The contrasting view, that the syntax of a language
can only be determined by conventional machinery going beyond simple associations of names with objects, I shall call the

theory that *syntax is constructed*. There are obvious correspondences between this pair of theories and the theories of natural and constructed nameables which we discussed in Part 1.

But now, it seems to me that Schlick, in adopting this view, has inadvertently relinquished his hold on the central—and correct—insight of the *Tractatus*. The structure of a sentence—that structure which makes the difference between a proposition and a name—cannot, as Schlick himself has earlier forcibly argued, be an *ad hoc* representation of some set of external relationships holding between things in the world, for the simple reason that we can construct new sentences. A mere portrait of the world, for all its isomorphy with what it portrays, has no generative potential. This is why, in the *Tractatus*, propositional 'pictures' are pictures of configurations whose possibility in guaranteed by the essential nature of *dingen*'— the substance of the world', as Wittgenstein calls them. The *Tractatus* solves the problem of the generative potential of language by writing it, as it were, into the metaphysical constitution of the world. But *some* solution is essential.

Moreover, how are we, on Schlick's final view, to locate the objects with which the names in our sentences are correlated? The same difficulties over natural nameables with which we earlier confronted Farrell, now arise for Schlick. How can we successfully indicate or 'gesture' towards, the referent of a name? One possible solution would be to augment our gesture with some account of the logical type of the name being defined. If we know that 'red' is a *colour*-word we shall know, perhaps, that we are to consider a given paradigm object from the point of view of which colour it exhibits, and not from any other point of view. But to know this sort of fact about the logical type of a term involves knowing its use in discourse. And to know its use in discourse is to know the meaning of the sentences in which it occurs. But on Schlick's final view we cannot know the meaning of sentences until we know the referents of the names which they contain. We are trapped in a vicious circle.

PART 3
A Model of Colour Naming

3. A Model of Colour Naming

I

Criticism is always easier than construction. We must ourselves face the question: How do we locate referents for names, and in particular for colour names? I want to begin by constructing a schematic outline of a possible answer to this question.

Let us, for the time being, drop the idea that our experience offers us an array of natural nameables, sufficiently clearly individuated by the conditions of our prelinguistic perceptual sensibility to serve as attachment points for associative linkages between names and the world. Let us suppose instead that the limits of application of a name are determined by some fairly elaborate set of prescriptive rules or procedures which we apply to our experience.

We must suppose, of course, that our experience is structured in *some* way, otherwise we could hardly specify the rules in question, but we suppose that it is not structured into natural nameables. In other words, the structure of our experience is not, in its virgin state, replete with linguistic significances which we can *tap*, as it were, merely by plugging a set of names into certain ready-made points in the structure by means of ostensive definition or some other associative procedure. The structure of experience does not simply metamorphose itself into the structure of language at the drop of a few thousand ostensive definitions.

We will suppose instead that the prescriptive rules which,

by operating in certain ways upon our experiential field, determine the limits of application of general terms within that field, produce, *given what happens to be true of the objects and structures with which we are presented by our prelinguistic perceptual sensibility*, the result that the terms so defined have certain privileges of occurrence in discourse and not others (have, in other words, a certain logical grammar). This comes about because of the way in which the rules governing the application of terms operate in conjunction with other sets of linguistic rules in the construction (or, to use a fashionable term drawn from linguistics) the generation, of sentences.

On this view the logical grammar (the use) of terms in a language is not a direct reflection of relationships holding in nature between the points in our experience with which names are associated. It is something quite separate from the structure of experience in this sense, for it is the outcome of the way in which a complex set of prescriptive rules operates in practise, given *the way in which experience is structured to begin with* (i.e. prelinguistically).

The theory at which we arrived a few pages ago as a result of developing ideas borrowed from Schlick and the *Tractatus* makes both objects of reference and syntactic structures into given features of our experience. On the theory whose programmatic outlines we have just developed, objects of reference and syntactic structures are linguistic entities. No doubt our experience is also divided into naturally individuated objects and structures, but these objects and structures have no linguistic significance in themselves and do not stand in any simple associative relationship to any linguistic entities. Linguistic entities are *constructed* in the sense that their individuation involves the application to the naturally individuated objects and structures of experience of complex systems of prescriptive rules.

The two theories might be represented schematically as follows:

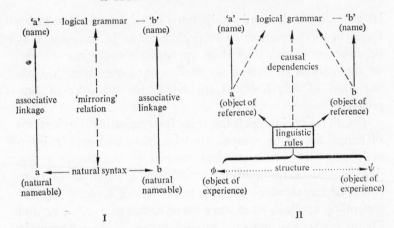

On Theory I now, it seems, as we saw a few pages ago, logically impossible for language to get off the ground. In order
to identify the referents of names I need—in order to know
what *sort* of name I am dealing with—to know the logical
behaviour of the names in question in sentences; but in order
to know this I must attach a sense to the sentences in question
and I cannot do this until I know the referents of the names
contained in them.

Theory II avoids this problem. The difficulty arises on Theory
I because Theory I represents the task of learning a language
as that of acquiring a grasp of two relationships (the relationship between a name and its referent, and the relationships of
possibility of co-occurrence in sentences which constitute the
logical grammar of a name), neither of which is accessible
without a prior grasp of the other. They are, moreover, relationships which it would hardly be possible to explain to someone
who did not already know, in a quite general way, what sort
of thing a language is; who was not already, that is, master of
a language. I shall call such relationships *linguistic relationships*.
On Theory II, however, what has to be grasped in learning a
language is neither a relationship between name and object of
reference nor a set of restrictions on co-occurrence in discourse;

i.e. not a linguistic relationship, but a set of rules for generating linguistic performances. The performances in question may be either sentences uttered in appropriate conditions of use, or applications of names: we shall confine ourselves throughout most of this book to the latter, for the sake of simplicity.[1]

The situation in which the rules for generating applications of names has to be grasped contains *three* elements in interaction. (1) The structure and content of the learner's prelinguistic (or extralinguistic) experience; (2) the set of rules which he has constructed, or is in process of constructing, for generating applicatons of some set of names n_1, n_2, . . ., n_n: and (3) the observable usage of other speakers of the language in applying n_1, n_2, . . ., n_n. The learner has to arrive at a set of rules which will generate applications of names which are consistently in conformity with (3) and in so doing has to locate the elements and structures of (1) upon which the rules in question are to operate.

This kind of problem is one which human beings find no great difficulty in solving. We learn how to ride bicycles, tie knots or play the oboe largely by trying to match the performances of others. No doubt such capacities require explanation, but we are not called upon to supply it. The important thing, from our point of view, about Theory II, is that it enables us to specify what has to be learned, in learning to apply names, without our having to make use, in giving the specification, of any *linguistic* notions; that is, of any notions which require reference to the experience of using a language if they are to be explained. We don't, that is, have to mention the relationship between a name and its referent. The learner who has successfully arrived at a set of rules for generating applications of colour terms will find that *the outcome of operating these rules* is that he uses

---

[1] An account of the relationship between naming and sentence generation will be found in my *Meaning and Structure*, Harper and Row, New York and London, 1972.

colour terms within limits of application matching those which the terms in question possess in the usage of other speakers. He can therefore say if he likes that he 'knows the meaning of colour words' or, if he is in a philosophical mood, he can say, meaning the same thing, that he 'can identify the referents of colour terms'. But 'the referents of colour terms' are not to be identified with the elements of his experience which enter into (1) above, for—we suppose—the rules which comprise (2) are not rules stipulating associative linkages between colour names and the elements in question. And hence the elements in question are not referents of names, nor, for that matter, are they *linguistic* entities of any description.

There is thus no difficulty in supposing, on Theory II, that the observable usage of other speakers provides adequate criteria of identification both for the rules (2) which the learner is trying to grasp, and the elements and structures in his experience (1) upon which the rules operate. Indeed it is evidently a condition of our being able to learn a language that the usage of other speakers should provide adequate criteria of identification for (1) and (2): a point which, as we shall see later, can be turned to effective use against certain forms of epistemological scepticism. We are debarred from this supposition, on Theory I, by the fact that Theory I represents the learner of language as having to grasp, *sequentially*, relationships which can only be grasped *in co-ordination with one another*, and by the fact that the relationships in question are, if the theory is correct, *linguistic relationships* in the sense which we defined a moment ago.

And, in addition Theory II meets the criterion of adequacy specified by (CA_1): it explains what must be learned in requiring a linguistic concept—reference of general names—without covert appeal to any presumed ability to use that or any other linguistic concept.

Finally, a theory of type II evades the necessity for a Tractarian distinction between what can be said and what can only be shown. If the limits of significant concatenation are determined by rules of language there is an obvious and sound reason why we do not require a further range of entities to account for the significance of the rules themselves. It is, quite simply, that the 'significance' of a rule is guaranteed by the possibility of obeying it: of carrying out the operation which it prescribes. An ill-formed rule is not a rule (whereas a semantically ill-formed sentence may still be a—grammatically well-formed—sentence). But if, on the other hand, what determines the limits of significant concatenation is thought of as the natural 'syntactic' articulations of experience, then we are in difficulties. For if the 'structural' relationships in question genuinely characterize experience it is hard to see why we should not formulate sentences in English, or any other language, asserting this fact. But then it really will be necessary to appeal to a further range of relationships of 'logical structure' in order to determine the limits of significant concatenation for these sentences. Thus, it appears, we can only avoid a vicious regress by denying in the teeth of common sense that the sentences in question do not express propositions: that the relationships which comprise 'logical structure' cannot, indeed, be expressed in language, but only 'show themselves in the logic of language.'

Theory II, however, exists so far only as a mere schematic programme. What I shall do in Part 3 is to try to fill in this schema in detail for the case of colour terms. I have introduced it here in schematic form because I have found by experience that it is difficult to develop the methodology and the detail of the theory simultaneously without creating a good deal of unnecessary confusion in readers' minds: the detail, as we shall see, is quite complicated enough on its own. I shall try in developing it to keep it tied to the schema presented above by occasional methodological asides.

What I hope to get out of this theory is, as hinted earlier, a set of new general arguments against scepticism about our knowlege of the content of other people's experience. It weakens my case to confine the argument, as I shall do, very largely to colour experience and colour terms. But I am not so much concerned with systematic completeness as with getting a certain type of argument against scepticism off the ground, and here I think the advantages of simplicity gained by confining the argument to one sensory modality are overwhelming. I shall try to suggest ways of extending the argument to other sensory modalities later on, but the suggestions will be very sketchy, and I must in any case confess to scarcely having begun to attack the problems presented by the logic of other modalities. But then, part of what I shall try to show here is that a sensory modality is necessarily *sui generis*.

II

What determines the limits of application of colour terms: 'red', 'pink', 'white', for example? We have seen that these limits are not completely determined by the nature of our extralinguistic perceptual experience. We must then, ourselves specify rules which determine the limits of application of such terms, which hence become terms denoting constructed nameables. But how? We cannot suppose, for example, that the limits of reference of such a word are determined simply by enumeration of exemplary objects to which the word is to be applied: that is, by a series of instructions of the following type:

R_1 *This$_1$* is to be called 'red'
R_2 *This$_2$* is to be called 'red'
R_n *This$_n$* is to be called 'red' . . .,

where the successive uses of the demonstrative correspond to the ostensive indication of various objects exhibiting red colour presentations. While it is perhaps intuitively obvious that this is so, the reasons why it is so are sufficiently complex and interesting to be worth stating briefly. In terms of our earlier discussion the trouble with this suggestion is simply that it gives us a term which applies, by the very nature of the rule governing its use, only to the members of a list or repertory of antecedently fixed membership, so that it would be impossible for someone to whom a particular colour presentation had not been expressly designated as falling within the limits of application of 'red', during the period when he was learning the use of the term, to recognize that presentation as one to which the term 'red' applies on coming across it for the first time later on. But while this is indeed a sufficient reason for rejecting the suggestion, it is not the most important or interesting one. If I can define the limits of application of 'red' by enumerating colour presentations it follows that I must be able to point to coloured objects *as exemplars of redness*. But it is, among other things, precisely the notion of referring to something, ostensively or otherwise, as an exemplar of colour, that we wish to elucidate. If my hearers, that is, can grasp that whatever sign or gesture I use to enumerate colours has the function of referring to things *qua* coloured things, they must already have grasped a meaning rule which enables them to put that construction on my performance; in other words the concept 'colour' must already be functioning in our common language before I can enumerate colours for their benefit.

We can put this in another way. If I point to my shoe, to the sun and to a smoke-ring and say 'All these things are *blik*', I have not, so far, defined the class of entities to which '*blik*' refers; and I have failed to do so because my performance has not furnished my hearers with any means of determining of any future entity with which they might become acquainted whether it was *blik* or not. If I enlarge upon my definition in such a way that it becomes clear that for me *blik* means, for example, 'curved', then my hearers will no longer be nonplussed, since they will in that case have been able to extract from my performance a rule for deciding of things whether they are *blik* or not. But then it is the rule, and not the enumeration of paradigm cases of correct application, which gives a meaning to *bilk*.[2] In the absence of such a rule, indeed, *bilk* is not a general term, but at most a proper name which, like *James* or *Arabella*, belongs to (not 'designates') more than one individual.

These two objections to a nominalist account of naming are manifestly connected. If I have a rule which determines the limits of application of a general term T then I can recognize things which did not figure in any array of exemplars by reference to which a teacher, or 'the linguistic community' taught me the meaning of T as things to which T applies. And if I cannot do this, then, since in that case I can have no rule for determining the limits of application of T, the expression which substitutes 'in my language' for the dummy expression T is not a general term at all, and indeed not an expression *in my language*, or any language, for no explanation of the meaning of a general term has, *ex hypothesi*, been given; enumeration of exemplars being, not a mode of explaining the meaning of a general term but (unless it functions as a means of identifying a rule), merely a kind of logical joke about, or parody of, such explanations.

Noam Chomsky and, as we have seen, Wittgenstein and Schlick before him, have suggested that the essential feature of a natural language, which differentiates language from other systems of communication, resides in the possibility of creativity in language use: that is, in the capacity which a speaker of a natural language possesses to produce and to understand sentences which are as new to him as to his hearers; which are generated by a process of rule-following and not merely drawn from a rote-memorized internal list or repertoire labelled 'acceptable English sentences for sundry occasions'. In Part 1 we extended this notion to naming, or rather to the process of

---

[2] Similar points are made by Julius Kovesi, *Moral Notions,* Routledge and Kegan Paul, 1967, I. 1–5; and by W. and M. Kneale in *The Development of Logic,* Oxford, 1962, p. 598 et seq., in arguing against Russell's theory of logically proper names.

applying names; and we suggested that the process of attaching colour names to colour presentations was in fact creative in this sense. If the above arguments are correct then this is not merely a contingent fact about colour-names, or about the English language: if I cannot apply a general term to individual[3] exemplars other than those to which its application has been expressly licensed by some finite ostensive procedure, then I have no rule for determining the limits of application of that term; but then, *a fortiori*, I have no general term.

It is no evasion of this argument to say that general terms acquire meaning by being associated not with 'individual' exemplars but with universals, and that a universal is a class of 'natural resemblances'. For, as we have seen, the natural resemblances of things cannot determine the limits of application of a word. To call a thing red is no doubt to *employ* its resemblances to other things in the process of applying the linguistic rules which determine that the term 'red' is correctly to be applied to that thing; but it is not to *point at* an abstract entity of a certain sort (a class of natural resemblances), for which the term 'red' is an associative label, and which manifests itself in (or something of the sort: the difficulties of specifying this relationship are well known) the particular which we assert to be red.

III

Consider an observer presented with an array of colour samples exhibiting different colour presentations. We can ask him to execute at least the following two sorts of performance.

P(1) Saying, or indicating by some appropriately arranged behavioural response, which of the samples seem to

---

[3] What constitutes an *individual* exemplar is, of course, determined by the logic of the general term in question, if its meaning has been adequately specified.

exhibit identical colour presentations and which distinct colour presentations.

$P(2)$ Arranging the colour samples so that they form, as far as possible, a continuously graded sequence of related colour presentations; for example, a sequence running from greens, through blue-greens to blues, with each hue successively a little more blue than the last.

We can compare the performances of different observers equally objectively in either case. Thus, for example, we could represent each observer's performance as a sequence of numbers corresponding to numbered colour samples: the results of tests of the ability to execute $P(1)$ would thus appear as a sequence of ordered pairs of numbers, while the results of tests of the ability to perform $P(2)$ would appear as a sequence of ordered n-tuples, where n is the number of discriminable hues represented among the samples.

It seems *prima facie* probable that most people asked to perform $P(2)$ would arrange a given set of samples in the same order: colour samples are frequently arranged in this way (for example, colour 'wheels' and charts, painters' samples, etc.) and there is general interpersonal agreement about the continuity of such arrangements: discontinuities (a greener blue suddenly intruding at the wrong point in a sequence of progressively bluer green-blues, for example) are remarked upon separate occasions by individuals who cannot reasonably be supposed to be colluding with one another with intent to deceive, and so forth.

What all this establishes is that there can be—and indeed is—intersubjective agreement about the existence of what Schlick calls 'a comprehensive system of shades' or an 'order of colours'. More is involved, of course, than a simple linear sequence of hues. The question of what types of relationship subsist between colour presentations has received a good deal of attention since the eighteenth century, much of it centred on the attempt to discover the geometry of a diagram capable of accommodating, in sequential order, all possible colour presentations. It is generally accepted that such a diagram must take the form of a three-dimensional array or colour solid, and most colour theorists would argue that the best colour solid has the form of a double cone.[4]

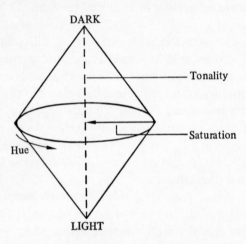

The vertical axis of the figure corresponds to a degree of tonality: the relative darkness or lightness with which a hue is presented in a given colour presentation (successively darker shades can be obtained by mixing greater and greater quantities of black with the same colour pigment). The radii of the central circle correspond to degree of saturation, or relative weakness or strength with which a hue is presented (different degrees of saturation can be obtained by diluting pigments with water

---

[4] A discovery due to Wilhelm Runge (1777–1810) and variously adapted by later theorists. See, e.g. *The Colour Primer*, ed. Faber Birren, Van Nostrand-Reinhold, 1969.

There exists a good many manuals and handbooks expounding the technicalities of the various 'colour solids' (e.g., those due to Ostwald or Munsell) and their associated systems of colour description. It is as well to look at several, as terminologies and modes of exposition of notions like saturation differ confusingly.

or white pigment). Hues at maximum saturation and median degree of tonality are arranged in sequence around the periphery of the central circle.

We thus have three dimensions upon which colour presentations colours can be arranged: saturation, tonality and hue. 'Metallic' colours introduce further slight complications which we need not bother with here.

It is important to see that these distinctions, and the fairly complex vocabulary for the description of colour presentations which they make possible, are not a part of the physiology or psychology of vision. They belong, not to the scientific explanation of colour vision, but to what one might call the descriptive phenomenology of colour experience. Philosophers writing about colour experience have paid singularly little attention to the logical structure of this vocabulary, but nonetheless it is, we shall see, of quite considerable philosophical importance.

One or two further facts about our colour experience need to be borne in mind. Not all 'colours' in the sense of colour presentations, are visible in spectral light however finely it is divided. There are many 'non-spectral' colours including all browns and pinks, olive greens, and others, which can be produced only by manipulating pigments. Finally 'brightness' is sometimes used as a synonym for 'tonality' but may also refer (i) to the actual intensity of the light emitted from the coloured surface or (ii) to the 'subjective' appearance of greater brilliance possessed by some spectral colours. Thus:

> Brightness is a function of colour. If we shine lights of different colours but the same intensity into the eyes, the colours at the middle of the spectrum will look brighter than those at the ends ... the curve being known as the spectral luminosity curve.[5]

I shall from now on speak of the total array of relationships exhibited within the colour solid as *the colour array*.

[5] R. L. Gregory, *The Eye and the Brain*, p. 77.

The problem of specifying limits of application for determinate colour terms—which I shall henceforward refer to as 'colour names'—can be formulated in this way: the colour array is a continuum: our use of colour names on the other hand is discontinuous, although its discontinuity is of a fairly complex type which, for example, allows joint application of some pairs of colour terms (e.g. green-blue) to the same colour presentation while rigorously excluding joint application of some other pairs (e.g., pink-yellow). The fact that, in our discourse about colour, our use of colour words faithfully observes these complex discontinuities, can, it seems to me, only be understood in one way. As speakers of the same natural language we possess in common a grasp of some set of rules which, by rendering certain features of our colour experience rather than others semantically criterial, impose a grid of linguistic distinctions upon the essentially seamless and continuous fabric of that experience, and enables us to generate judgements about the applicability, (inapplicability, joint applicability) of colour terms to particular colour presentations which agree with the judgements of our fellow native speakers precisely because their judgements also issue from the application of (are generated by) the same system of linguistic rules.

Our job is to try now to get at the nature of this shared rule system. I think it is obvious from what we have said already that two suggestions which immediately present themselves will not do. The rules cannot be *arbitrary* in the sense that they affix names to particular presentations, viz:

R_1 : Let presentation P_1 take the name 'blue'
R_2 : Let presentation P_2 take the name 'blue' and the name 'green'
R_n : Let presentation P_n . . .

and so on; if only because in that case any of these stipulations would be revocable without prejudice to the others. However attractive a property this kind of extensionality may appear in the light of our metaphysical impulses, it is not one which our colour vocabulary possesses. I cannot—in a sense of 'cannot' which we shall shortly try to elucidate—have 'blue' and 'orange' mean what they normally mean but nonetheless *choose* to say that turquoises, for example, are blue-orange in hue. The intensionality of our ascriptions of colour names entails, it seems to me, that the rules which generate such descriptions are not arbitrary in the above sense, but somehow *yield* ascriptions of particular colour terms to particular colour presentations without expressly *specifying* each such ascription.

We cannot, again, specify the limits of application of a particular colour term by presenting one or more paradigms of the correct application of the term. What people have in mind when they propose this as a mode of 'definition' of the 'basic' terms of language of immediate sensory description is, I think, a procedure like the following, roughly analogous to mathematical induction.

Step 1: 'Blue' is correctly applied to *these* colour presentations, $P_1, P_2, \ldots, P_n$

Step 2: 'Blue' is correctly applied to any colour presentation which resembles other presentations to which 'blue' is applied in just the degree in which they resemble each other.

Such a procedure, in effect, construes a 'natural resemblance' as a special relationship linking a determinate set of colour presentations: a relationship which can be identified by presenting as a paradigm two or more presentations related in the required way. If this were so we could define each colour name separately, without mentioning any other colour name. But, as we have already seen, such a procedure simply allows us to go on expanding the range of colour presentations that we must, if we follow the rules, count as 'blue', in effect depriving us of any criterion for denying the applicability of the term.

We can get beyond this impasse, I think, if we take seriously the idea that the rules for applying colour names must somehow divide up the continuum of the colour array. We can do this, obviously, if we take two or more distinct points on the colour array and assign colour names according to whether a particular presentation is closer to (more like) the presentation which occupies one or another of these points. Let us call the points in question 'name-bases'. We thus get a procedure, not for 'defining' a single colour term, but for semantically partitioning the entire colour array between the fields of application of at least two colour names. We can represent this procedure schematically as follows:

[P_2] *Step* (*1*) : Let P_1, P_2, . . ., P_n be name-bases.

Step (*2*) : Let the phonemic strings S_1, S_2, . . ., S_n be introduced in one-one co-ordination with P_1, P_2, . . ., P_n as colour names.

Step (*3*) : For any colour presentation P_0 determine which of P_1, P_2, . . ., P_n it most resembles, say P_m. The colour name associated with P_m is then the *name of primary application* to P_0.

The colour array does, that is, offer us a basis for making judgements of relative degree of resemblance between colour presentations, and this can serve as a basis for establishing limits of application for colour names provided we introduce colour names, not singly, but in co-ordinated sets. To this extent talk of 'natural resemblances' is justified.

Thus, if we choose name-bases suitably,[6] a procedure of this type will partition the colour array exhaustively, in the sense that each colour presentation will receive through the operation of the device, at least one colour name. It will receive it, more-

---

[6] 'Suitably' of course is a crucial word. P_0 may be such that it resembles P_1 no more than it resembles P_2 or any other name bases. We shall return to this point later.

over, not by direct stipulation of a name but as the outcome of operating a device the fundamental specifications of which make no assignment of names to colour presentations, other than the initial assignment of names to name-bases. The model satisfies one of the theoretical constraints which bear upon any theory of colour-naming: it shows how it can be possible for a speaker of a language, confronted by a new hue (a newly discovered chemical dyestuff with a unique hue never before seen in nature, for example) with which he could hence, by the very fact of its newness, never have been taught to *associate* a name, nonetheless to be able to put a name to that hue which agrees with that put to it independently by other speakers of the language. We shall see later that it also explains among other things, the 'overlap' of colour terms in actual usage.

To associate a name with a name-base according to the procedure in step 2 of /P_2/ is not in itself to *define* the name in question *by association*, or to *bestow a name on* the colour presentation in question. This is because the limits of application of the colour names introduced into the language by the device schematically represented by /P_2/ are given by the operation of /P_1/ as a whole and not by step 2 in isolation. In carrying out step 2, that is, we have not introduced any colour-names into the language, but merely carried out a necessary preliminary step in the process of introducing colour names. /P_2/ is thus not an associative model of colour naming. Similarly, it is not abstractionist: the referent of a colour name is not, according to our model, *what is common to* paradigm objects to which that name is applicable: certainly it is not *what is common to* name-bases, since only one name-base need be given to identify a particular colour.

We can now see, I think, how to begin filling in the schematic programme of Part 3 §I. /P_2/ is, in effect, a procedure for generating a certain set of linguistic performances: applications of the colour names $S_1, S_2, \ldots, S_n$ (we can easily imagine circumstances in which this performance might be executed: for example, a teacher points to various coloured objects: a learner produces an appropriate colour name). What the learner has to derive from the observed usage of his elders is a set of procedures, capable of being applied to his experience, which will generate a pattern of applications of terms matching theirs. He will be led to a suitable set of procedures if he simply tries to match the colour name assignments made in his hearing by his elders, calling 'red' anything relatively more similar to things that they call 'red', 'blue' anything relatively more similar to things that they call 'blue' and so on. He will in effect be taking their assignments of colour names as locating name-bases and applying Step (3) of $/P_2/$, using his errors to correct his practice as he goes along.

It might seem that we are here blandly ignoring an obvious objection on which we harped *ad nauseam* earlier on in the disscussion. How does the learner know that the names in question are colour names? Why should he, in looking for a procedure for generating applications of those particular names, fix on a procedure which, in effect, partitions the colour array? Doesn't this require him to possess a prior insight into the use in discourse of the names in discourse which, as we have repeatedly insisted, he cannot possibly possess?

The short answer is that the learner can only arrive at a set of procedures which generate a pattern of name applications in conformity with the usage of other native speakers if the rules in question operate on certain aspects of his experience rather than others. If he tries to construct rules which operate on anything but the colour array—on shape, or brightness, or texture, say, he will simply not succeed in matching his elders' linguistic performances. And there are only so many sets of pervasive features of his experience upon which the rules he is seeking can operate. Trial and error will soon produce modest successes in anticipating other peoples' applications of names and the development of his nascent rule-system on the lines suggested by these successes will single out colour as the field of application of colour language. Rules, experience and the observed usage of other speakers are thus held in a continuous tension which serves to identify error and idiosyncrasy either in the form of the rules or in the ways in which they operate on the extralinguistic structures and objects given in experience.

It might now be objected, however, that the same thing could be said for a plain, traditional account of naming in terms of ostensive definition. Surely if the usage of other speakers can be supposed to locate the field of application of colour language it can be supposed to single out the referents of colour terms. This, however, is to miss the force of the original objection as it bears upon associative theories of naming. It is because what the learner has to locate, if the theory of ostensive definition is correct, is the *referent* of a term, that the objection holds against the theory. Referents, as our earlier arguments showed, are linguistic entities. To know the referent of a term—that 'red' refers to 'a colour', for example, it to have grasped a linguistic relationship. Hence I cannot know that a term being defined for me by someone is a colour term unless I am already familiar with the notion of colours as forming a certain category of referents, and this involves my already understanding the logic of colour words and how they operate in discourse.

It is important to see that attention to the usage of other speakers cannot help the learner in this plight. He cannot test his hypotheses about the workings of language against their usage until—obviously enough—he has some hypotheses to test. But on the associative model any hypothesis he can frame will take the form of a tentative linkage between a name and some referent: but as we have seen, this presupposes that he already knows a great deal about language. We can only get out of this difficulty if we can represent the learner as acquiring a grasp of procedures which *issue in* linguistic performances, but which are such that we can understand how a learner comes to grasp them without attributing to him a prior grasp of any essentially linguistic concepts or relationships.

IV

Our model as so far formulated stands open, however, to an empirical objection: that is seems to make the way in which we divide up the colour array for semantic purposes a matter of entirely arbitrary choice. That is, it suggests that the boundaries of what we recognize, for puposes of linguistic reference, as 'colour' can be drawn more or less where we please within the space of the colour solid. This is, indeed, a view which has in the past been very popular with linguistics and anthropologists, who have subscribed to a doctrine of linguistic relativism in respect of colour, according to which each language adopts its own, entirely idiosyncratic set of boundaries, which need thus bear no systematic relationship to the set of boundaries chosen by any other language, although, of course, accidental coincidences between the limits of application of particular colour names in different languages may from time to time occur and will be more likely to occur in languages of the same linguistic family. This view has never held the field unchallenged however, and recently quite strong evidence has accumulated which suggests that it is wrong. Two American anthropologists, Brent Berlin and Paul Kay,[7] have established that if informants are asked to select, from a standard array of colour samples, the best, most typical examples of the colours named by their native terminology, the results do not, even with languages of very different linguistic families, yield a random scatter of focal point across the entire extent of the colour array. Instead, focal points in the twenty languages examined cluster about eleven narrowly restricted areas (including black and white) on the colour chart,[8] the area in question being those which also include the foci of the English colour terms 'white', 'black', 'pink', 'orange', 'yellow', 'brown', 'green', 'blue', 'purple'.

[7] Brent Berlin and Paul Kay, *Basic Colour Terms*. University of California Press, Berkeley and Los Angeles, 1969.

[8] See the chart on pp. 8–9, Berlin and Kay, op. cit.

Berlin and Kay are concerned with what they call 'basic colour terms'. Their criteria for the status of a basic colour term involve eliminating terms which for one reason or another can be classed as non-basic: for example, descriptive phrases like 'the colour of bananas', qualified colour terms ('salmon pink'), colour terms whose sphere of application falls wholly within the sphere of another colour term (scarlet, light red) and so on, basic terms being the residuum.

Not all languages possess basic colour terms associated with all of these foci. Some languages possess, indeed, as few as two basic colour terms. Berlin and Kay's data suggests that a complex relationship holds between the number of colour terms a language possesses and the particular colour foci around which that language organises the colour array. Thus, if a language has only two basic colour terms they are 'black' and 'white', if three, 'black', 'white' and 'red', if four, either green or yellow, if five, the other member of the green-yellow pair, and so on, according to the following scheme:[9]

$$
\begin{bmatrix} \text{white} \\ \text{black} \end{bmatrix} < \begin{bmatrix} \text{red} \end{bmatrix} < \begin{bmatrix} \text{green} \\ \text{yellow} \end{bmatrix} < \begin{bmatrix} \text{blue} \end{bmatrix} < \begin{bmatrix} \text{brown} \end{bmatrix} < \begin{bmatrix} \text{purple} \\ \text{pink} \\ \text{orange} \\ \text{grey} \end{bmatrix}
$$

The apparent universality of these colour categories might be explained if colours were natural nameables: if the limits of application of 'red', for example, were determined independently of all linguistic conventions (except of course, the associative conventions necessary to link name and nameable) by the nature of experience. But quite apart from the arguments

[9] Taken from Berlin and Kay, op. cit., p. 4. The expression '$a<b$' here signifies that a is present in any language in which b is present and also in some language in which b is not present.

which have led us to reject this view in the foregoing, others of Berlin and Kay's findings are inconsistent with it.

Thus they find;[10] for example, that whereas the placement of foci by different informants and by the same informant at different times is highly consistent, the placement of category boundaries, even by the same informant from one occasion to another, is highly unreliable. Secondly, what is constant from language to language is the category *focus*, and not the domain of colour presentations which a given focus governs. Every language examined by Berlin and Kay possesses a colour vocabulary which partitions the colour array exhaustively between the fields of application of its basic colour terms, irrespective of how many basic colour terms it contains; and earlier ethnological and linguistic studies of colour naming in some 70 further languages appear to confirm these results. Thus some languages partition the colour array between 'white' and 'black'. These terms have their foci approximately where English speakers would place them but the domain of application of 'white' extends over all light hues, that of black over all dark hues, so that the colour solid is, roughly speaking, horizontally bisected near its upper end.[11] In languages which add a third basic colour term, 'red'; 'red' covers all reds, oranges, most yellows, browns, pinks, and purples, including violet, the remainder of the colour array still continuing to be partitioned between 'white' and 'black'. Further additions to the vocabulary of basic colour terms continue to restrict the domains of application of these primitive terms.

It might be possible to explain these observations by appeal to differences in the ability of different human populations to perceive colour, but no evidence for such differences exists, while there exists a good deal of evidence[12] which seems to show

---

[10] Op. cit. 1.6.   [11] Op. cit., p. 17 et seq.

[12] See, e.g. Lenneberg, Eric H., *Biological Foundations of Language*, N. Y. John Wiley and Sons, 1967; Post, Richard H., 'Population Differences in Visual Acuity', *Eugenics Quarterly*, 9.4: 189–212, 1962.

that speakers of languages which segment the colour array in radically different ways nonetheless show no significant differences of performance in colour discrimination tests.[13]

These results seem to be of some philosophical interest. If correct, they seem to show that the partitioning of the colour array for purposes of reference is subject to constraints which are independent of language and culture. At the same time, these constraints allow different languages to construct referents for colour terms in radically different ways: 'red' in a three-colour-term language can hardly be said to *mean the same as* or to *refer to the same colour* as 'red' in English, since the two terms have radically different limits of application.

I am not primarily concerned to defend the validity of Berlin's and Kay's results.[14] They seem to me to have an impressively documented case, but I am not a linguist or an anthropologist; and in any case the attempt to enter into linguistic or anthropological questions for their own sake at this point would lead me far from my main purpose. What I do want to argue is that the model of colour naming which we are in process of constructing yields a very simple and direct explanation of some of Berlin's and Kay's universal features of colour vocabularies. In particular, the consistent identity of colour foci seems to derive, on our model, directly from the inspectable character of the colour array as a particular structure of directly perceivable internal relationships. In so far, then, as it suggests a familiar and clearly defined source for some of the universal constraints

[13] The idea of partitioning the colour universe between black and white often produces, I find, a kind of mental vertigo (are these people colour blind? or mad?) until one realizes that one obvious and simple solution is that the rules which serve to partition the colour array for purposes of naming in their language operate solely upon tonality and not at all upon hue.

[14] A defence of relativity in colour naming, with an attempt to represent Berlin and Kay's results as an artifact of their use of chemical dyestuffs in colour samples, has already appeared (N. B. McNeill, 'Colour and Colour Terminology', *J. Linguistics*, v. 8, No. 1, February 1972) and no doubt the discussion among ethnolinguistics will continue.

which Berlin and Kay claim to have discovered, thus giving us reason to expect colour vocabularies to reveal the effects of these constraints, our model offers a certain amount of corroborative support for their thesis.

I do not think that the arguments which I shall now present throw much light on the systematic correlation which Berlin and Kay claim to have discovered between the number of basic colour terms a language possesses and the identity of the foci to which the terms in question correspond, and which they interpret as a developmental sequence. But I shall try to show that they do throw some light on, and perhaps explain, the fact that the foci of colour terms are constantly located in certain restricted areas of the colour array, the fact that the latter are located where they are, and the fact that while the foci of colour terms are very easy to point to, informants find it hard to set precise limits to the fields of application of colour terms.

If we try, using a two-dimensional representation of the colour array constructed by selecting hues at some reasonably close standard interval and displaying them in measured degrees of saturation and tone,[15] to assign values to two of our dummy name-bases P_m, P_n; we shall find that not all assignments will actually result in an exhaustive division of the colour array. Thus, if we choose two almost adjacent presentations, two medium blues for example, we shall find when we come to apply step (3) that the question, Is P_o more like P_m or P_n? admits, for all but a very few presentations clustered about P_m and P_n, of no definite answer. Orange is not more like Oxford blue than it is like Cambridge blue, and vice-versa. If we wish to get two assignments which do divide the colour array exhaustively, then we shall have to move the sites of the assignments

---

[15] E.g., a colour chart of the sort produced for scientific purposes by the Munsell Colour Company. Ideally I would have wished to include an actual colour chart in this book, but the cost proved prohibitive. A chart of the kind I have in mind can be found in Berlin and Kay, *Basic Colour Terms*, op. cit.

apart, and I think it can be seen by inspecting an actual colour chart of the sort described above that the closest possible choice which allows of actual division will put one name-base in the blue-green segment of the colour array and the other name-base in the purple-red-orange-yellow segment.

What I am saying comes, roughly speaking, to this: if we try to divide up the colour array exhaustively into fields of application of colour names by using procedure $/P_2/$, we find, when we try to apply this procedure to colours as we actually experience them, that we cannot get an optimally exhaustive division (or, for two name-bases, any division at all) unless we observe certain limitations upon our choice of name-bases.

The 'cannot' in the last sentence might be thought to require explanation. Are we supposed to be dealing with some category of necessary relationships? And doesn't this smack of metaphysics? The short answer to the first of these questions is, yes; and to the second: I fear so. The relations between colours are, as philosophers have traditionally believed and Schlick rightly affirms, 'internal' ones: what this means we shall see later on. And our argument will turn out, in the end, to have a metaphysical conclusion, despite its unpromising initial obsession with the nature of linguistic convention. For the moment however, we must defer these questions to Part 4, and allow the argument to continue.

Let us suppose that we respond to the constraints upon the application of Step 1 imposed by the actual perceived character of the colour array, and place one name-base in the purple-to-yellow segment of the array, and the other in the green-to-blue segment. The exact location, within these broad segments, of the name-bases chosen to illustrate the use of colour terms to a particular learner on a particular occasion is, as we shall see, quite unimportant.

I think it is evident that, wherever we have placed the name-bases P_m and P_n, the question 'Is P more like P_m or P_n?', will never yield a definite and clear-cut answer for *every* colour presentation in the colour array. Exhaustive division is a theoretical limit to which only a relatively more or less close approximation is possible, precisely because we are dealing with a qualitative continuum.[16] If we are correct, the placing of P_m and P_n respectively in the orange-red-purple and the blue-green segments of the array yields an optional approximation to exhaustive division, but there will, even so, remain some presentations which seem to resemble P_m quite as much as they resemble P_n. The rules of $/P_2/$, as so far formulated, give us no license for applying any colour name to those intermediate cases. A natural extension of $/P_2/$, however gives us:

Step (4) : If step (3) yields no decision for a given P_o and a given pair of name-bases P_m, P_n; then P_o takes both of the colour-names associated with P_m and P_n.

We now have a linguistic procedure which imposes, by a purely linguistic manoeuvre, an artificial exhaustiveness on the division of the colour array, and ensures that any colour presentation will receive, by the operation of the rules of the language of which $/P_2/$ is a part of the semantic description a definite specification in the form of one or at most two colour names. The augmented version of $/P_2/$ is in fact a simple algorithm which works by a stepwise matching procedure, in which a given colour presentation is compared with successive pairs of name bases, one member of each pair being lost at each matching by the operation of Step (3) until either a single name-base or a pair of name bases neither of which can be dropped by appeal to Step (3) remain, in either of which cases a colour specification can immediately be read off by applying either Step (2) or Steps (2) and (4) in conjunction. It is to be noticed, moreover, that the ability to apply Step (3) presupposes no

[16] Or a series of discriminations so fine that they can be regarded as constituting a continuum for our purposes.

psychological capacity other than the primitive (and operationally specifiable) capacity to arrange colour presentations into order of hue which we introduced at the beginning of Part II. For it is obviously the case that if, and only if, we can recognize that one colour presentation is relatively more similar in hue to a second than to a third we can arrange colour presentations in a series according to gradation of hue.

For two name-bases, now, the augmented version of $/P_2/$ ($/P_2/^1$) will yield a large set of presentations labelled S_n, a large set labelled S_m and a small set labelled with the dual designation $S_m S_n$. These sets are not, obviously, internally disordered. For, given that we can arrange the colour array in a series according to gradation of hue, it follows trivially that each presentation in the array must be assignable to a definite place by the *degree* of similarity which it bears to one or more presentations chosen arbitrarily as bases. It follows that where we have two bases, each presentation in the array will correspond to a determinate value for the degree of similarity which it bears to each base. The situation is one which we could represent abstractly, that is, by assigning to each presentation a two-digit number such that each digit varies from 1 to 10; presentations around the mid-point (5:5) being those receiving the joint designation $S_m S_n$. We can thus introduce a further refinement of $/P_2/$: we can provide for the characterization of a colour presentation by naming both its predominant hue and the hue which qualifies it, as for example in English, 'a reddish yellow', 'a greenish blue', etc.

Let us now consider the actual partitioning of the colour array produced by siting one name-base amongst the presentations which make up the red-yellow-orange-brown-purple-segment of the colour array and one name-base amongst the blues and greens, associating with the two name-bases respectively the dummy colour names 'orange' and (stealing a leaf from Nelson Goodman's book) 'grue'. It is clear that many roranges will, as a result of this partitioning, be more or less grue-ish roranges, although for reasons which would appear, in terms of a more expanded grid of partitionings of the colour array such as that governing ordinary English usage, rather disparate. Thus, olive-browns may appear grueish roranges because they tend to merge into olive-greens; purples will be grueish roranges because of their affinity with bluish violets, and so on. It will now be possible to ask 'Which are the most characteristic —the most typical—roranges?' taking this in the sense of 'Which are the least grueish roranges'; and an obvious procedure will lie to hand for arriving at an answer to this question: namely, tracing back all lines of diminishing grueness until they meet at a common point, or rather at a common small area of the colour array. It seems to me, now, clear from inspection of the colour array that what we shall arrive at by carrying out this procedure is the area of 'pure reds' in which Berlin and Kay's informants, irrespective of language, locate the focus of the term 'red' (that 'rorange' approximates closely in use to Berlin and Kay's primitive red' as that term is used in languages possessing three colour terms); and that we shall arrive at this location for the colour category 'pure rorange' irrespective of whereabouts within the rorange portion of the colour array we sited the name-base by reference to which we originally introduced the concept *rorange* into our language.

What I am suggesting, in other words, is that the notion of a pure colour is not a stipulative but a constructed concept, in the sense that the location of 'pure' cases of a given colour is not a primitive move in setting up a language, but is the outcome of the operation of systems of rules governing the introduction into our language of other, and hence more primitive concepts. It is certainly a fact that it is possible to exhibit exemplary cases of red, green, and so on, and to exhibit further for each colour a range of cases in which the hue present 'in a pure form' in the exemplary cases is gradually diluted with other hues. Philosophers have been misled by this fact into taking the view either that a colour is a real universal, of which particular colour presentations can 'partake' in various degrees, or else that it is a 'class of resemblances' whose limits can be defined by stipulating a paradigm case or cases, resemblance to which is to constitute the criterion for the application of the corresponding colour name. If this latter view were true it would be difficult to understand why speakers of widely differing languages should use colour terms having the same foci, or indeed why colour-term foci, being stipulative in origin should not differ from dialect to dialect, or even from speaker to speaker, within a language. If the above arguments are correct, however, what we call an exemplary, or typical, case of a colour cannot be a matter to be determined by the stipulation of a basic rule of language, but is the outcome of the interaction between, on the one hand, the nature of those rules of our language which have as their object the exhaustive partitioning of the colour array into fields of application of colour names, and, on the other hand, the perceived nature of the colour array itself. The exigencies of this interaction are such, if we are right, that we can only divide the colour array for a given number of name-bases by siting those bases within certain limits, and once we have done this, the rules by which we generate judgements concerning the relative weight of the hue affinities present in a given colour presentation yield, whether we will or no, a certain location for the pure cases of each colour so introduced, no matter where we stipulated the location of the original exemplary presentations by reference to which we introduced the colour names in question. *Red* is not, in Locke's sense, a 'nominal essence', although, for that matter, it is not a 'real' one either.

Similar things, I think can be said of 'grue'. Grue will include yellow-greens, greens, blue-greens and blues. At two points then, we shall find presentations which, by the application of augmented $/R_2/$, take the designation rorange grues: namely, in ordinary English, yellowish greens and violet blues. If we follow back the lines of decreasing rorangeness observable in this sub-array, we shall be led to pure green along the yellow-green-green axis and along the blue-green green axis while pure and violet blues appear as a range of steadily more (rorange grues) rorangish blue-greens. We now have two constructed foci for 'rorange' and 'grue' respectively, and these foci dominate fields of application of those terms which exhaustively partition the colour array. We can now treat these foci as name-bases relative to which we can introduce further name-bases. The constraints which operate at this level are the same as those which operate at the level of the initial introduction of name-bases: we must, that is, adopt a minimum spacing of the sites of foci and new name-bases if we are to achieve by the application of $/R_2/$ Step (3) an actual partitioning of one of the fields of application governed by 'rorange' or 'grue'. Thus, for example the location of a name base in the orange-yellow segment of the rorange meets this condition: if we call this name base 'rellow' we can achieve by reference to it an optimal approximation to exhaustive partitioning of (old) rorange colour presentations between (new, residual) rorange and rellow. Within the class of rellow presentations we shall now be able to distinguish between rorange, rellows (oranges) and grue rellows (greenish yellows) and the lines of decreasing rorangeness and grueness will intersect at (in our terms) the pure yellows. Readers can verify for themselves that the foci of blue, purple, pink, brown, turquoise and orange can be constructed in the same way.

Let us now try to relate this briefly to the regularities observed by Berlin and Kay. First, the uniformity of location of foci and the identity of their locations now appear, given the uniformity (or virtual uniformity) of human colour perception, as trivial consequences of the use of such procedures as $/P_1/$ and $/P_2/$ to accomplish the tasks of individuation necessary for the introduction into a language of reference to colour. Similarly, the ease with which the exemplary cases of a colour can be produced and their uniformity from speaker to speaker is a consequence of the fact that each speaker is identifying exemplary cases by applying a set of linguistic rules which he shares with other speakers of the same language, and which not unnaturally yield similar results when applied to similar sensory material. The difficulty of assigning clear boundaries to the fields of application of colour terms is, again, a result of the character of the rules which partition the colour array, and in particular of the fact that a diminished relative resemblance to one name-base persists in colour presentations whose predominating relative resemblance is to another.

Our account throws less light on the apparent correlation between number of colour terms and identity of associated foci. According to Berlin and Kay, in all languages with two colour terms, the foci of these terms are black and white, and these foci dominate respectively all dark and all light hues. That is, at this point colour language is based upon the tonality series and not at all upon the hue series. Languages with three terms introduce a term associated with the red focus, black and white continuing to partition the blue-to-green segment of the colour array. Our account allows us to predict (a) that the hue introduced by the first hue-based colour term will be either 'red' or 'green', and (b) that the area of the colour array dominated by the red focus will be approximately what it is in such languages, but offers no explanation of why 'red' rather than 'green' should be the first hue-series based term to appear. Similarly we can explain why, if a focus appears next in the blue-green area, it will be green, but not why a focus should appear there rather than in the red area. This is perhaps forgivable, since the second hue-based term introduced by a four-term language, may, it appears, correspond to either the green or yellow focus. But then we have no explanation of why yellow should appear before brown, which can equally be arrived at by partitioning our 'rorange' (Berlin and Kay's primitive 'red') in the manner suggested. The same thing goes for the apparently regular introduction of 'blue' before 'brown' or 'orange'. But no doubt other

factors than those described by our model enter into the con-
stuction of actual colour vocabularies.

V

We have now partly filled in the details of the schematic theory
of Part II, and in so doing we have begun to give a definite content to the notion of a constructed nameable. The rules of
$/R_2/^1$ do not establish associative linkages between colour
names and things 'in the world'. Nonetheless they establish
limits of application for colour terms. It is only because we
have a set of rules that do this that we can speak of 'colours' as
distinct from 'colour presentations'. Colour presentations are
given in experience—that is, they can be individuated by extra-
linguistic criteria. The notion of a 'colour' on the other hand
can be explained only by way of explaining the rules by which
we confer limits of application on colour names; and these are
linguistic rules.

Colour names, as we shall see in a moment, possess a logical
grammar: a set of possibilities of co-occurrence with each other
and with other sorts of term in sentential contexts. This logical
grammar is the joint outcome of (i) the nature of the rules
which compose $/P_2/^1$, and (ii) the content and structure of the
perceptual material—the colour array—upon which the rules
operate. But the logical grammar of colour words is something
quite separate from the structure of the colour array. Logical
grammar is a set of linguistic relationships, whereas the structures of the colour array consists of a set of internal relationships
between perceptual qualities. Once we see (1) that the structure
of sentences and the structure of the world are radically different
kinds of structure, and (2) how it is that the former arises as
the outcome of a set of rules which operate in various ways
upon the latter, there remains little temptation to fuse the two
levels of structure by introducing the notion of a 'fact' or a

'state of affairs' as a structural analogue, in the extra-linguistic world, of the sentence. Sentences have structure, ultimately, because the world has structure, but the world is not structured into naturally individuated wholes corresponding to sentences. We saw in discussing the *Tractatus* that this temptation arises in the first place largely from the need to find some explanation of the possibility of constructing new sentences. We shall return to this point later.

VI

We need to give some account, however, not just of the concept of 'a colour' and of the concepts of 'red', 'blue', 'green', etc., but of the concept 'colour'. What is it that enables us to recognize new colour presentations as new instances of the universal 'being coloured'? Judgements of this sort, like judgements of redness or greenness, must be *generated*. They cannot, precisely because they concern new presentations, be founded upon antecedent associations of the term 'coloured' with a specific set of objects. One ancient device for securing such generality of reference is by appeal to common properties. But a colour presentation is, as Locke would have said, simple. It cannot be analysed further into elements, and thus it cannot have elements in common with other colour presentations. And if we say that it has at least the property of being coloured in common with other presentations we are arguing in a circle: what we wish to understand is how we assign the predicate 'being coloured'.

Hume has the following footnote in the chapter of the *Treatise* that deals with abstract ideas:

It is evident, that even different simple ideas may have a similarity or resemblance to each other; nor is it necessary that the point or circumstance of resemblance should be distinct or separable from that in which they differ. *Blue* and *green* are different simple ideas, but are more resembling than *blue* and *scarlet;* though their perfect simplicity excludes all possibility of separation or distinction. It is the same case with particular sounds, and tastes, and smells. These admit of infinite resemblances upon the general appearance and comparison, without having any common circumstances the same. And of this we may be certain, even from the very abstract terms *simple idea.* They comprehend all simple ideas under them. These resemble each other in their simplicity. And yet from their very nature, which excludes all composition, this circumstance, in which they resemble, is not distinguishable or separable from the rest. It is the same case with all the degrees in any quality. They are all resembling, and yet the quality, in any individual, is not distinct from the degrees.[17]

What Hume has relegated to a footnote seems to me to be the key to our present problem. If we are to be able to group simple sensory presentations into general categories at all, it can only be by appeal to unanalysable relationships of the type which Hume discusses.

We thus seem forced to adopt the view that what entitles us to refer to something as coloured is the possibility of assigning that thing to some place in the complex system of internal relationships that characterize the colour array. Colour is, then, simply the aspect of things under which they stand in these relationships to one another.

The relationships in question are certainly not brought into existence by the rules of our language: they characterize features of our experience. It looks, therefore, as though colour is a kind of natural nameable; as if we speak of 'colour' we gesture towards a set of relationships whose limits are determined by the nature of our experience and not by language. This will not do as it stands, however. To recognize something as coloured is

---

[17] David Hume, *A Treatise of Human Nature*, Bk I. Part I, VII, footnote.

manifestly, in our view, *not* to recognize it as linked, *by virtue of an association*, to the word 'colour'. It is to see the possibility of relating the thing in question to other things so that they form part of a certain sort of system. We can put this in another way if we see that, in our view, a set of objects presented as paradigms of what is meant by 'being coloured' would not function *separately* as paradigms of 'colouredness' but only *conjointly* as paradigms of a certain sort of relationship.

Recognizing the possibility of a relationship can be regarded equally well as recognizing the possibility of an operation: of actually setting things in a certain kind of order or sequence. One way of stating the difference between the present view of the logic of 'colour' and an associative-ostensive view, would be to say that in our view 'colour' corresponds not to a *thing* (an object of reference) but to an operation. We can say if we like that colour is operationally defined: that the limits of application of 'colour' are determined by the practical limits of applicability of the operation in question (that is, the operation of setting things—colour samples, say / by reference to the colour presentations they exhibit, in the three dimensional array of relationships represented by the colour solid. But to say this of course, only to say that to be coloured is to be capable of being assigned to a place on the colour array.

What we seem to be saying is that the individuation of the fundamental modalities of perception depends upon the fact that the items falling under these modalities exhibit continuous systems of internal relationships. This is plausible enough for colours and perhaps sounds (pitch, intensity, harmony etc.), but what about taste, smell, and touch, for example? Surely, many of the items falling under these modalities must be regarded as logically discrete. What relates the taste of a pineapple to the taste of salt, for example, or the smell of new mown hay to the smell of hyacinths? I shall not attempt to give an adequate answer to this objection here, although I think that it could be answered. If I were to continue the discussion in this direction I should take as a text the following quotation from Lévi-Strauss.

Modern chemistry reduces the variety of tastes and smells to different combinations of five elements: carbon, hydrogen, oxygen, sulphur and nitrogen. By means of tables of the presence and absence of the elements and estimates of proportions and minimum amounts necessary for them to be perceptible, it succeeds in accounting for differences and resemblances which were previously excluded from its field on account of their 'secondary' character. These connexions and distinctions *are however no surprise to our aesthetic sense*. On the contrary they increase its scope and understanding by supplying a basis for the associations *it already divined* and at the same time one is better able to understand why and in what conditions it should have been possible to discover such associations solely by the use of intuitive methods. Thus to a logic of sensations tobacco smoke might be the intersection of two groups, one also containing broiled meat and brown crusts of bread (which are like it in being composed of nitrogen) and the other one to which cheese, beer and honey belong on account of the presence of diacetyl. Wild cherries, cinnamon, vanilla and sherry are grouped together by the intellect as well as the senses, while the closely related smells of wintergreen, lavender and bananas are to be explained by the presence of ester. On intuitive grounds alone we might group onions, garlic, cabbage, turnips, radishes and mustard together even though botany separates liliaceae and crucifers. In confirmation of the evidence of the senses, chemistry shows that these different families are united on another plane: they contain sulphur.[18]

The 'logic of sensation' which peers from between the lines of

[18] Claude Lévi-Strauss, *The Savage Mind*, Weidenfeld and Nicolson, 1966, p. 12 (my italics).

this quotation (Lévi-Strauss is after quite other game) would clearly be a logic of internal relations. A start towards tracing out this notion in linguistic terms might be to examine the categories 'sweet', 'bitter', 'aromatic', which seems to correspond to axes upon which tastes or smells can be arranged rather than to particular tastes or smells.

VII

By way of postscript to this part it may be worthwhile to anticipate one further objection. What I have said might be interpreted as an attempt to say *what goes on in us psychologically when we apply colour terms*, in which case what I say must seem manifestly absurd. As philosophers sometimes emphasise *ad nauseam*, I need not have anything at all going on in my head when I say things like 'There's a red bus'; let alone the preposterous apparatus of comprehensive colour charts marked with name-bases, etc., etc., which my account seems to suggest.

I hereby disclaim any such ambition to become a scene-painter for Ryle's 'shadowy theatre of the mind'. My concern is with the logic of colour names, and not with the psychology of their use. On the other hand, the fact that we do not need to bear in mind a formal and explicit statement of the criteria of application of a term on every occasion when we use it, does not mean that the term has no criteria of application which can be formally stated.

PART 4

The Limits of Scepticism

4. The Limits of Scepticism

I

We can now, at length, return to the distinction between form
and content, and its apparent epistemological consequences.
We have been arguing, primarily, against the view that the
referents of the terms in the colour vocabulary are natural
nameables, or what comes in the end, as we saw at the outset
of Part 3, to the same thing, the view that the logical grammar
of colour language is simply a representation, or map of the
natural syntax of colour experience (that the natural syntax of
colour wholly determines the limits of significant concatenation
so far as colour language is concerned, without any contribu-
tion from the character of the linguistic rules governing reference to colour). On either view, it is necessary and sufficient
for the understanding of both the sense of a sentence about
colour and the reference of the names which it contains that
the hearer should be able to correlate the structure of the sentence with the structure of his experience. The content of
experience is irrelevant to this process of correlation. It follows
that it would be logically possible for the content of experience
to vary radically from person to person, without this variation
having the slightest effect upon the use of language or upon the
smooth progress of communication by means of language, provided that the structure of everyone's experience remains the
same. I shall call this property of such postulated arrays of sensory contents 'discourse neutrality'. The logical possibility of the

existence of discourse neutral discrepancies of colour vision, for example, is one obvious consequence of the inexpressibility thesis.

The consequence of admitting the logical possibility of discourse neutral discrepancies in the content of different persons' experience are, of course, sceptical. It seems very plausible to say that if you cannot (logically cannot, that is) reveal to me by the way in which you use language the radical way in which the content of your experience differs from mine, then there is no way in which you could reveal it to me (or, by the same token, come to know of it yourself), for I cannot inspect your experiences, nor you mine. We are left, it seems with that perennial product of sceptical argument, an apparently theoretically well-specified class of empirically undecidable contingent propositions. This conclusion is philosophically disagreeable; to empiricists as much as to anybody else. One can, of course, attempt as Schlick at one point does, and as Smart and Farrell do in a different way, to rob it of its sting by denying any empirical cash-value to the term 'content'. But this move is not merely counter-intuitive, but self-defeating: it leaves us with an account of the meaning of colour words constructed in terms either of discrimination or of structural correspondence, but renders us not merely unable to say, but unable to ask, what observers in discrimination tests are discriminating between ('hanks of wool' or 'numbered areas enclosed by lines inscribed upon a sheet of paper' will not do as an answer) or what the structural features of experience are structural features of; and hence makes it impossible to see why the existence of a distinction between the form and the content of experience should in the first place have presented itself and its associated problems to philosophers.

We shall explore a different path. To begin with, it will be worthwhile to examine the precise nature of the scepticism to which we are led by the form-content distinction and the apparent demonstration which it offers of the logical possibility of discourse neutral discrepancies in the content of different persons' experience. What is involved, it seems to me, in this sort of scepticism, is a denial of any epistemological significance, so far as the confirmation or disconfirmation of judgements about parity of content of experience is concerned, to the fact that we are able to understand one another when we describe the content of our immediate sensory experience. I shall call this *scepticism about relevance*. It is quite different from another form of scepticism, which I shall call *scepticism about completeness*. We can get at the difference by examining some of the ways in which the kind of claim about discrepancies of colour vision which psychological testers make concerning colour-blind and normal subjects differs from the sort of claims made by the relevance sceptic about his postulated discourse neutral discrepancies of colour vision.

Colour-blind people discriminate fewer colours than their fellows. There exist tests capable of revealing, more or less conclusively, the existence of such incapacities. One such, for example, consists of a set of cards printed with dots of colour of equal size and interval. The colours of the dots vary, so that to the normally sighted one card may appear, for example, to exhibit a '2', displayed as a pattern of pink dots against a background of light green dots; whereas to a red-green colour-blind person the dots which, for the normally sighted, constitute the '2' are indistinguishable in hue from those which compose the background, so that the card appears featureless.

Such tests are conclusive, of course, only *ceteris paribus*. They demonstrate the ability, or the lack of it, to make certain colour discriminations, provided we can exclude the possibility of collusion, extrasensory perception of one sort or another, use of marked cards, advice by Socratic demons, and so on and so forth. But there are relevant procedures to whose successful outcome we can appeal in support of the claim that these possibilities can reasonably be excluded. Scepticism about actual cases of the exclusion of one or another such possibility is one kind of completeness scepticism. Another kind, for example, might concern the question whether the normality of a person's colour vision is demonstrated by his satisfying all the tests for presently known varieties of colour-blindness: perhaps more discriminating and subtle tests might reveal some slight difference, of a type previously unknown to science, between my discriminatory abilities and those of others. Doubts of this kind, like those of the former kind, can be raised at any point in the development of science: they constitute no more than a quite reasonable and proper unwillingness to regard the current state of knowledge as exhaustive. Such 'scepticism' is quite consistent with a belief that the orderly extension of knowledge is possible: indeed, it is only in a context of acceptance of the existence of a vast web of actual and possible considerations relevant to the acceptance or rejection of claims to knowledge of various sorts that such doubts can be formulated.

Relevance scepticism, on the other hand, consists precisely in the belief that certain propositions, which we can formulate and in some sense 'understand the meaning of', are nevertheless completely and absolutely dissevered from this web of cognitive relevancies, in the sense that nothing whatsoever *could* be relevant, even *ceteris paribus*, to establishing their truth, or the truth of their negations; the 'could' being presumed to have the force of logical impossibility. Thus, in the particular case which we have been considering, the nub of the sceptic's case lies in the claim that the fact that we can understand each other's discourse about colour and ourselves produce discourse about colour which others understand, is simply irrelevant to the question whether we perceive the same colour qualia as other people, since even if we did not, a mere structural uniformity, holding between radically disparate universes of qualia, might suffice to preserve all the appearances of verbal communication.

Relevance scepticism seems to me to be far more disturbing than completeness scepticism. It attacks the foundations of our belief, not just in the relative completeness or accuracy of communication among men, but in its reality. When we talk to other human beings we normally assume that the content of experience is publicly available to all the parties to the conversation. As Wittgenstein says somewhere in the *Investigations*, I do not normally think of blueness as something interior to me; something to be indicated by a reflexive gesture of Cartesian introspection. I think of it as something external to myself: if I want to point at something blue I point not at the inward landscape of my mind, but at the sky. And I take the blueness of the sky to be something which others can perceive just as well as I can.

Philosophers who have been influenced, not so much by Wittgenstein's later work as by the currently dominant physicalist-cum-positivist interpretation of Wittgenstein's later work, are apt to display a marked discomfort at the suggestion that scepticism about the possiblity of communicating about content presents us with problems of any great philosophical interest or importance: something that one ought to get seriously worried about. Indeed, they regard such worry as implicitly selling important philosophical passes. A reader of an earlier draft of this book wrote in the margin of the previous page, 'But most of how I see it (the world) is structure. And once you've grasped this you can stop being disturbed. And earlier he wrote, 'What is structure at one level is content at another. The sceptic is right about the *lowest* level. But so what?' Another reader insisted that to entertain worries about what I have called relevance scepticism is to implicitly grant that 'experience of objects, persons, etc. is compounded of experience of *qualia*', which it is not.

These objections are proper and serious. They stem from a just conviction that no sound epistemology can be erected upon the foundation of an empiricism which identifies the fundamental data of knowledge as private deliverances—private in the sense of being logically inaccessible to anyone except their possessor—of experience, and the fundamental operation by which knowledge is constructed as the compounding or aggregating of such deliverances. The fatal blow to such theories is rightly thought to have been struck by Wittgenstein's demonstration that the ostensive indication of a private event or object cannot suffice to confer meaning upon any expression in a language, not even a 'basic' or 'fundamental' expression; and that therefore the processes by which we confer meaning upon expresions in our language must have to do entirely with events or objects which are not private in the above sense. The effect of this, along with many other forces in English-speaking philosophy, has been, as we all know very well, to make philosophers turn their attention to the actual use of concepts in discourse, and to the actual ways in which we are enabled to make reference of one sort or another to things of different logical types (mental states and acts, persons, material objects, intentions, motives, for example). And such investigations do indeed reveal that our conceptual scheme depends on a very complex fabric of distinctions which can be represented, in terms of the present discussion as, broadly speaking, structural.

I don't want to attack either the value or the general rightheadedness of these developments in philosophy. Both seem to me to be beyond question. Indeed most of our discussion so far has betrayed, implicitly and explicitly, its own derivation from this very tradition in philosophy.

But I am not at all sure that we need to abandon the cammunicability of content to the sceptic as the price of avoiding an associationistic and atomistic epistemology. Philosophers who believe that this price must be paid believe it because they accept that content is private. But this is exactly what I shall be questioning in the remainder of this book. My conviction that we ought to be worried by scepticism about the communicability of content thus springs, not from a failure to see that scepticism can be successfully demolished on many other fronts, but from the conviction that such demolitions, though sound and valuable, do not go far enough: that the sceptic can be defeated on this front as well, and that his defeat here will reveal some important philosophical truths.

There is, however, another motive for taking relevance scepticism seriously. An important part of my belief that other people are persons and not just cunningly contrived robots[1] rests in turn on the belief that their experience has, broadly speaking, the same content as mine. Thus, if I say to you even something as simple as that from where I am sitting I can see a cloudless blue sky through the branches of a willow tree in new leaf, what I often[2] intend is that you should be able, if you wish, to visualize this scene *as I see it*. If I have to take into account the possibility that certain structural elements common to the disparate ways in which we perceive the world will be abstracted by you from the syntactic and semantic structure of my utterance and, as Schlick would say, 'filled in' by you in such a way as to yield either a visualized scene with a totally different content, or perhaps not a visualized scene at all, but a neurologically encoded representation of the structure in question, then both the above beliefs are radically undermined. The presumption that we inhabit a common sensory world, that when we exclaim at the sky seen through young willow leaves we are exclaiming *at the same structure of contents* collapses, and its place is taken by a vivid and depressing sense of personal isolation: an isolation which is more hopeless than mere loneliness because it is logically, and not merely practically, irremediable.[3] There are of course other ways of arriving

---

[1] My admission of a distinction here will no doubt annoy physicalists, behaviourists and computer engineers. This is too bad.

[2] Of course, it is equally often the case that neither the mechanisms nor the aims of communication involve visualisation.

[3] For some minds this feeling can be a quite potent means of weakening the sense of immediate contact with the lives and personal experience of other people; a sense which for various reasons I think one ought to wish to see strengthened.

at similar conclusions, but they are mostly, I think, less elegant, and less immediately persuasive, than the seeming demonstration of the discourse-neutrality of content.

The distinction between doubts which are in principle capable of being settled by some extension of what ordinary scientific and commonsense criteria entitle us to call knowledge, and 'philosophical' doubts which acquire their peculiar irresolubility from the fact that they call in question the ordinary criteria of knowledge is, of course, a commonplace of the analytic tradition in philosophy; and it is equally common to argue that no sense can be attached to philosophical doubts precisely because they call into question the ordinary criteria not merely of the truth but of the meaning of propositions. This is a view with which I have some sympathy: indeed, the anti-sceptical arguments which I am about to put forward are, very generally speaking, of this type. The trouble with such views as they are usually put forward is that they leave quite obscure, except perhaps, for a few rough examples or analogies, accompanied by a general appeal to linguistic intuition, the mechanism by which 'criteria' or 'rules' determine 'meanings'. It is thus not easy to show the exact nature of the incoherency which infects the sceptic's hypotheses, or to distinguish them clearly from related propositions which pretty clearly do make sense.

The general outline of the solution which I shall now offer is as follows. Relevance scepticism depends upon establishing the logical independence of logical grammar and the limits of application of names from considerations bearing upon the qualitative character of content.

As we saw earlier, Farrell is only enabled to accomplish this feat of logical disconnexion by implausibly identifying the referents of names with indiscriminable recurrents. Schlick tries to perform the same feat by (1) showing that the referents of names are identified by matching the structures of proposition with the natural syntax of our experience, and (2) distinguishing within experience between a level of external relationships *expressed* by sentences and a level of internal relationships which somehow determine the *possibility* of certain sentence structures. If both these moves worked, then indeed the referent of a name would be identified merely as a particular location within a fabric of internal and external relationships: whatever content happened to occupy, for a given observer, the location in question would be, *for him*, the object referred to by that name, but the identity of the content in question would be quite indifferent from the point of view of the workings of language.

We have abandoned both the idea that there are natural nameables, and the idea that a sense can be given to a sentence by correlating its structure with 'the structure of a fact'; that is with some part of that prelinguistically given structure of experience which Schlick in effect construes as constituting a 'natural syntax'.

Against these models we can set the model which we developed in Part 3. On this model the limits of application of a colour name and its privileges of occurrence in discourse both result from the mode of operation of a set of conventional procedures for dividing up the colour array. The colour array itself is a structured system: its structure provides the basis for the operation of the procedures which divide it up for purposes of linguistic reference. But the structure of the colour array is a structure of internal relationships; a fact noticed by both Schlick and Hume but from which neither drew the proper conclusion. This is, simply, that the structure of the colour array is logically inseperable from the content of colour presentations. The result is that if we imagine the content of our colour experience altered or transposed in any way, we can show that the operation of the ordinary procedures by means of which our language divides up the colour array would yield different outcomes from those which it normally yields, in the shape of different limits of application and different privileges of occurrence in discourse of colour names.

The operation of the procedures which conventionally divide up the colour array for purposes of reference is, in other words, *in principle revelatory of changes in content*. Moreover, we shall show that this logical inseparability of form and content is a necessary precondition for the existence of individuating criteria for colours; so that if form and content could indeed be prised apart in the way the sceptic proposes, it would not merely be the case that our colour language would allow individuating reference only to particular structures but not to particular contents: rather, we should possess no colour language at all.

II

We have now to establish these claims in detail. The relevance sceptic can make, it seems to me, two sorts of claim about possible discourse neutral discrepancies of colour vision. Suppose we have two observers, Smith and Jones. The sceptic can claim that if Smith sees colours normally (sees reds as reds, greens as greens, etc.) while Jones perceives *the same* hues as Smith but perceives these as systematically transposed in some way (e.g., sees greens where Smith sees reds, or something of the sort) then the resulting discrepancy of colour vision between Smith and Jones would be discourse-neutral. Or he can have it that Jones perceives no hue perceived by Smith, and vice-versa, but that each perceives a radically disparate set of presentations, such that neither set includes within itself any member of the other set; each set, however, displaying structural relations amongst its members identical to those displayed by the other set. For reasons which will become clear in a moment these two sorts of hypothesis are exclusive alternatives: they cannot be combined in any intermediate form.

An example of a claim of the first sort occurs in John Wisdom's *Other Minds*.[4] Wisdom says:

> Surely I can *imagine* that when I see red, white and blue he (Smith) sees black, green and yellow? ... Smith, of course, when asked the colours of the Union Jack replies 'Red, white and blue' because he has been taught to call the colours he then sees 'red', 'white' and 'blue'. But does he then see the same colours, red, white and blue as we see or does he see, say, black, green and yellow?

How real are these curious possibilities? I shall first state three general limiting conditions which transposition of the sort envisaged would have to overcome in order to satisfy quite minimal requirements for discourse-neutrality. I shall then list, with brief explanatory comments, three sorts of consideration, having to do with the character of the linguistic rules governing the application of colour words, any one of which seems to me to be altogether fatal to the idea that any such transposition might meet these conditions.

The general limiting conditions are as follows:

(1) *Preservation of discrimination relations.* No two colour samples discriminated by Smith must be indiscriminable to Jones, and vice-versa, other things (including the phenomena of colour-blindness) being equal.

(2) *Preservation of total numbers of discriminable presentations.* Smith must not discriminate more colour presentations than Jones, other things (including colour-blindness phenomena being equal.

(3) *Preservation of all dimensions of ordering of presentations.* The projected transposition must leave all gradations of hue, brightness and tone unaltered; i.e. whenever Smith sees a certain degree of difference of hue, or tone, or

4 John Wisdom, *Other Minds*, Blackwell, Oxford, 1956, p. 10.

brightness, Jones must see exactly the same degree of difference (with the usual *ceteris paribus* clause).

(3) means, in effect, that the sceptic must envisage transpositions within one 'dimension of colour' which are neutral with respect of the other two dimensions. This immediately rules out Wisdom's postulated transposition of black for red. For if Jones sees reds as (presumably uniformly) black he will make (what appear to Smith to be) red colour samples the termini of the scale of increasing tonality of every hue. Jones' scale of tonality for red will look particularly odd to Smith, since to him it will appear as a column of uniformly black samples topped by a single shade of red, the exact shade differing arbitrarily on different occasions when Jones is asked to construct a red tonality series.[5] Jones will nonetheless, construct tonality series normally except where red, or the last sample or two of the series for other colours (hues) are concerned.

There are, now, three sorts of consideration which prevent the sceptic's proposals from meeting the above conditions.

A. THE SEMANTIC TOPOLOGY OF THE COLOUR ARRAY

As we have seen, the result of choosing a successively greater number of name-bases, and locating foci within the fields of application of colour names generated by these name-bases, is to partition the colour array into a (smaller or greater) number of fields with more or less fuzzy boundaries. A colour presentation receives a colour name of primary application with greater or less certainty depending on its position with respect to these foci: passing from focal to less focal presentations invariably

[5] Incidentally, the difficulty of imagining a physiological mechanism which could account for the perception of uniform black samples as a range of reds is no argument against the sceptic, first, and most importantly because neither he nor we are doing psychology or physiology, but philosophy with at most a few linguistic overtones; and second, because, as Land's experiments with colour photography have recently demonstrated, there is very likely a good deal more to the physiology of colour vision than meets, so to speak, the eye.

brings us eventually to an area in which two colour names compete for primary application to the presentations in question: passing beyond this area changes the colour name of primary application. What I shall call a *semantic topology* of the colour array comprises the pattern formed by the fields of application of names into which the rules of a given natural language partition the colour array. It is clear that a particular set of name-bases determine a particular semantic topology—a particular pattern of fields of application of colour names. We can interpret a semantic topology either as a pattern of single and joint ascriptions of colour names or (less adequately) as an actual pattern of (more or less fuzzy) boundaries described within the volume of a colour solid.

The essential point of my argument, now, is that these are not stipulated but constructed boundaries. It follows that we cannot merely stipulate, as a basic 'rule of language' that a given semantic topology shall remain constant under reshufflings of the presentations which make up the colour array, since if the procedures which constructed that topology are applied to a different array of presentations they will construct a different topology. Hence, it seems to me, the relevance sceptic's proposal could not be feasible unless it were the case, at least, that the procedures which construct fields of application for colour names actually partitioned the colour array into topologically congruent volumes each of each contained exactly the same number of discriminable colour presentations (indiscriminable recurrents). For otherwise the same colour name would have a different field of application in Smith's usage from that which it had in Jones'.

It seems to me quite certain that this condition is not met by the colour vocabulary of English, and highly unlikely that it is met by the colour vocabulary of any language.

Berlin and Kay give the following diagram for the distribution of areas of primary colour names, in an eleven-term language such as English, over a two-dimensional colour chart

formed by taking forty equally spaced hues and displaying
them in eight degrees of tonality at maximum saturation (brightness).[6]

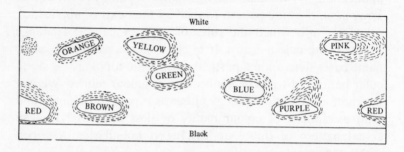

It is obvious at a glance, I think, that no rearrangement of
the presentations composing the chart will exchange any of
the areas of primary application of names without breaching
one or another of conditions (1)–(3). Two related points need
to be made here, the first concerning the shape and disposition
of fields of application, the second concerning the number of
discriminable presentations comprised in each. To begin with,
if we try to exchange limited groups of presentations for one
another, for example purples for browns, we shall find ourselves in trouble with the continuity of the hue series, which
will no longer be an even gradation without sharp breaks. Any
initially plausible transposition must, therefore, affect all hues
simultaneously; that is, must be representable as some shift or
rotation of the whole chart. If we rotate the chart about its
horizontal axis there will be a general shift upwards or down-
wards in the level at which foci are situated, and, in particular
one focus (brown) will occupy the position of two (orange and
yellow) in the unrotated chart, and vice versa. Moreover, we
shall find ourselves in difficulties with the tonality series, for
Jones' 'black' will correspond for him to the greatest pheno-

[6] A copy is given in Berlin and Kay's book. Extra copies can be obtained
from the University of California Press, Berkeley, California 94720.

menally apparent emission of light by samples, rather than, as for Smith, the least. Again, there is no vertical axis about which the areas of primary application of the eight colour (hue) names are symmetrically arranged, nor finally is there any way of achieving congruence by joining the two ends of the chart to form a cylinder and rotating that.

Secondly, inspection of such a chart reveals that the number of presentations within the field of application of a colour name at its most generous limits varies from name to name. We might attempt to fudge these numbers, and for that matter avoid some, at least, of the problems about the location of focal areas, by importing into Jones' phenomenal universe some colour presentations which do not occur in the chart as perceived by Smith. But all that this would achieve would be to breach the first and third of our general limiting conditions. For (a) it would mean that different discrimination relationships would obtain between the general body of colour samples available, *ceteris paribus*, to Smith and Jones (flowers, grass, the sky, dyes, etc.) and the two bodies of samples constituted by, respectively, the-chart-as-perceived-by-Jones and the-chart-as-perceived-by-Smith; and this will show up as soon as Smith and Jones start using such charts to identify colours. And (b) it would mean that the presentations on the chart would no longer be equally spaced in the three dimensions of hue, tonality and saturation: our fudging would show, indeed, as patches of looser or denser spacing.

I have stated these arguments in terms of a two-dimensional colour chart because of the difficulty of following, without an extensive apparatus of charts and samples, arguments conducted in terms of colour solids. But it is obvious, I think, that the sceptic has nothing to gain from a retreat to the colour solid: if there is no transposition of hues which will deal with the complexities of a two-dimensional array extracted in a systematic manner from the colour solid then, *a fortiori*, none will cope with a three-dimensional array.

B. THE HIERARCHICAL STRUCTURE OF COLOUR VOCABULARIES
Hume observes that '*Blue and green* are ... more resembling
than *blue* and *scarlet*, though their perfect simplicity excludes
all possibility of separation or distinction.' What Hume has
here stumbled upon is, if we are correct, the fundamental
principle by means of which we construct a common vocabulary
of colour concepts. By applying it we can partition the colour
array into a successively greater number of fields of application
of colour names. The later fields in this series are necessarily
split off from primordial fields: thus we can speak of an order
of hierarchical subordinations holding between themselves,
which corresponds, not to arbitrary semantic caprice, but to the
fact that the field of application of a subordinate colour name
would be, in a simpler and differently organised colour-vocabulary, included in the field of application dominated by the
focus of the superordinate colour name. For English these
relationships can, it seems to me, be represented as follows:

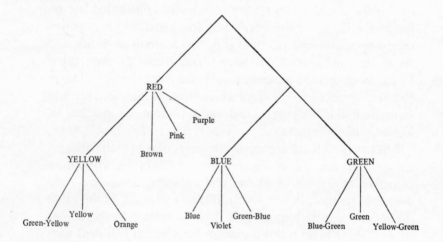

Once again I want to argue that these subordinations are not stipulated but generated: they are not *provided for* by 'the rules of our language', but flow from the interaction of these rules with sensory material to which they are applied. Hence, parity of the results of such application must be expressly preserved, in this respect as in others, by any transposition of hues for which discourse-neutrality is claimed. The difficulty in preserving parity is, now, that colour names are not merely hue-names: their fields of application do not, that is, segment merely the hue series but the three-dimensional colour space produced by the interaction of the hue series with the two other series which lie in the dimensions of saturation and tonality. The hue-series (the series of 'pure' hues red-purple-violet-blue-blue-green-green yellow-orange-red) might appear to be symmetrical in the required sense; that is to have two primary hues and two secondary, or intermediate hues on the red-resembling side of the colour-wheel, and the same number on the blue-green side. We distinguish at least two colours (brown and pink), however, which are not pure (spectral) hues, but are the result of desaturating spectral hues in different ways—in the case of pink by increasing the amount of white in a pure red, in the case of brown by increasing the amount of black to different degrees in reds, yellows or oranges.

Now, if we take into account brown and pink the hierarchical tree of colour names is asymmetrical: there are more colour-names on the red-yellow branch than on the blue-green branch. We can see how this will disrupt discourse-neutrality if we consider a transposition of colours achieved by rotating the (pure) hue series through 180°. We can represent this transposition as shown in the diagram on page 110.

When Smith directs Jones' attention to a sample of pink, now, what he will be directing Jones' attention to in Jones' perceptual universe is a sample of desaturated (pale) green. And similarly, when he directs Jones' attention to a sample of brown, what Jones will see will be either a dark green, or a

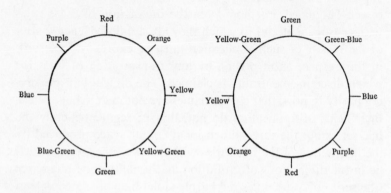

1. Smith   2. Jones

dark blue, or a dark blue-green. He will now be able to use the words 'brown' and 'pink', but only extensionally; that is, by applying *ad hoc* verbal substitution conventions of the form:

1. When *P* takes the description 'dark yellow', for 'dark yellow' may be substituted 'brown'
2. When *P* takes the description 'dark orange', for 'dark orange' may be substituted 'brown'.

.
.
.

etc.

Thus the form of the rules by means of which Jones generates ascriptions of 'brown' will be quite different from the form of those by which he generates ascriptions of other colour names and by which Smith generates ascriptions of all colour names including 'brown'. And there will be nothing to prevent Jones from commenting on this fact, by remarking for example, on the linguistic oddity in English which provides a special colour name for certain dark shades of red, yellow, and orange, when the shades in question have nothing in particular in common. In other words, the transposition produces a sort of lacuna, which must be filled by *ad hoc* stipulation of semantic equivalences, in the otherwise generative fabric of Jones' colour vocabulary. And similarly of course Jones will be inclined to say that dark blue, for example, is really a quite different colour from blue, and one more naturally related to dark green, and will express surprise that such presentations are linguistically assimilated by English to blue rather than to green; and complementary puzzles will exist for Smith in interpreting Jones' colour vocabulary if, as might eventually happen, Jones and his like invent one which sits better with the actual way in which they perceive colours.

A few moments' thought will show that similar impediments to discourse-neutrality will arise if we attempt more limited transpositions within the limits of the blue-green and red-yellow segments of the hue-series (for example, exchanging yellow for red while simultaneously—to avoid disrupting the order of the hue-series—exchanging blue for green).

C. JOINT ASCRIPTIONS OF COLOUR NAMES[7]

Some joint ascriptions of colour names in English refer to possible colours, viz. 'blue-green', 'reddish-yellow', 'blueish-violet'. Others, such as 'blueish-yellow', greenish-red', orangey-magenta', do not refer to possible colours: they are in some sense or other semantically ill-formed, or as Chomsky and some other generative grammarians would say 'semantically anomalous' expressions. If we are correct, the sense of 'possibility' which is applicable here is the sense in which it is not possible for a piece to traverse all the squares of a chessboard by

---

[7] See also my 'On Describing Colours', *Inquiry*, 1967.

making pawn's moves. What makes 'greenish red' semantically ill formed is merely that that expression is not in fact generated by the linguistic rules which generate ascriptions of colour names, when we apply them to the actual colour array perceived by us. It is thus quite idle to treat such propositions as 'there are no greenish reds' as expressing empirical propositions, and to speculate about an alleged contingent possibility of the perception, perhaps by beings with differently constituted sensory organs, of a red which, unlike any red perceived by poor mortal men, is greenish. What makes such speculations inappropriate is that we are not dealing with contingent possibilities; nor need we allow ourselves to be driven into such a position by the fear that if we reject it we shall have to admit 'there cannot be a greenish red' to the status of a synthetic *a priori* judgement. We are confronted merely with the possibilities of extracting certain results from certain specific name-generating devices, when these are applied to certain sensory material.

This is not to say that there are no conceivable circumstances under which the application of the ordinary rules of our language to altered sensory material would lead to the generation of expressions like 'reddish-green'. R. W. Pickford, an authority on colour vision, remarks[8] '... the tendency to exploit compound names for simple colours justifies our suspicion of colour vision defect. If a person is inclined to use the expression "reddish-green" for certain yellows he may be suspected of being partly red-green blind.' Later on he enlarges upon this point as follows:[9]

Edrige-Green has pointed out that certain red-green blind subjects may see a colour which they call 'reddish-green'. This must not be taken to mean that they see both the quali-

---

[8] *Individual Differences in Colour Vision*, Routledge and Kegan Paul, London, 1951, p. 5.
[9] Ibid., pp. 99–100.

ties of red and green as we see them but combined in one hue. No doubt the reddishness is more like what we should call orange, or even merely yellowish brown, and the greenishness is more like our olive or a desaturated yellow. Hence a colour to which we should apply the name fawn may to the colour-blind appear to combine the qualities he would call red and green, just as a purple may appear to us to combine qualities we should call red and blue. Thus he may use the term 'reddish-green' with fair frequency, as shown by Collins, and it is no more difficult to understand than the term 'reddish-blue' for ourselves.

Pickford assumes in this passage that the colour-blind are trying to apply consistently in the peculiar conditions of their own visual universe a system of colour concepts learned from the normally sighted. And indeed it is only on the hypothesis that we are dealing with a common system of semantic rules, which generate different verbal expressions depending upon the nature of the perceptual material to which it is applied, that the phenomena which Pickford describes become intelligible. If colour names were given meaning by one-one association with the members of a class of natural nameables, then, obviously, we should expect colour-blind people either to specify colours exactly as normally sighted people specify them, or else, where the colours that they are asked to put a name to are ones which they simply do not discriminate, to flounder and produce randomly assorted odd specifications, or else none at all. What we should, precisely, not expect is that they should produce, in a systematic and consistent way, specifications which normally sighted speakers would find semantically anomalous. But this, apparently, is what happens.

The possibilities of joint ascription of colour names offer, then, for by now familiar reasons, a further set of parities which must be preserved in any discourse-neutral transposition of colours. This excludes, for a start, any transposition which exchanges a 'psychological secondary' (purple, yellow-green, orange, blue-green. For then Jones would call red (purple to him) 'orange-purple' and so on. We might avoid this by the 180° transposition of the hue-circle canvassed in our discussion of (B). But here a further problem arises. It is a commonplace fact that mixing semi-transparent blue and yellow pigments produce green. This happens because any blue pigment reflects green as well as blue light: the superimposed yellow pigment acts as a complementary light filter, the light from it giving white light in conjunction with the blue light from the blue pigment, leaving the green light to be reflected unaltered from the surface to which the pigments are applied. Now, if colours are transposed in A's vision as we have suggested, he will see a pure blue which reflects some green light as a blue tinged with red and will call it a 'slightly greenish blue'. He will call 'pure blue' a blue with enough red in it (seen by him as green) to neutralize the green (which he sees as red). The result will be that he will agree that the mixture of blue and yellow pigments (which he sees as red) is 'green', but will engage in petty arguments with N as to which blues are 'pure', tending to describe as 'pure blues' those which N calls 'reddish blues', whereas the blue that N calls 'pure', he will be inclined to call 'greenish blues'. Once again it will not do for the sceptic to argue that 'pure' is a name taught by the presentation of certain paradigm colours to which the title 'pure' is affixed by arbitrary fiat, for as we have seen 'pure' is a term which receives a meaning not by a fundamental semantic stipulation but through the operation of pre-existing rules of the colour vocabulary, the rule for its use being that no colour ϕ which can be described as a ψ-ish ϕ is a pure ϕ, but that every other colour which can be described as a ϕ is a pure ϕ. Once again, if we can satisfy ourselves that Smith and Jones are using the same linguistic device, the fact that they are obtaining incompatible results by its use gives us grounds for concluding that they are applying it to different sensory material.

III

Let us suppose that the foregoing arguments really do show our ordinary convictions about each other's experience of colour to be invulnerable to, at least, the sort of relevance scepticism which turns up on postulating transposition of the colours which (so we assume everybody sees. It might still reasonably be asked whether we have shown anything of much philosophical importance. For we have so far shown nothing of interest *about* this sort of relevance scepticism. All that seems to have emerged, it may be said, from a rather wearisome maze of technicalities is that, given the nature of language (at least so far as this is represented by our chosen model), and given the nature of our colour experience, we happen *as a mere contingent matter of fact* to be invulnerable to this sort of scepticism. We have not at all shown that there is anything logically absurd or incoherent about even this limited variety of relevance scepticism, or that its claims might not be entirely valid and unanswerable with respect to a type of language and a type of colour experience different from our own.

To answer this objection we must return to our earlier discussions of the limits of significant discourse; of what it is that sets bounds to the application and significant combination and recombination of words. That we can arrange colour samples in order of hue, brightness and tonality, that we can learn the fields of application of colour names, that different observers can idependently put the same name to a sample of some new dyestuff of a hue unfamiliar to both or, what comes to the same thing, hover with the same degree of uncertainty between the same two alternative colour names, that different speakers locate the foci of the colour names of their language in the same areas of the colour array, that we recognize the same hierarchical order of relationships of relative similarity between colours (i.e. 'colours' in the sense of the referents of colour names), that our joint ascriptions of colour names run parallel: all these things both (i) furnish grounds for our belief that others see colours as we do, and (ii) constitute the manner in which, *de facto*, our language satisfies the necessary preconditions for the possession of criteria for the application and use of colour terms. Briefly, the main thesis which I wish to defend, one which seems to me of considerable philosophical importance, is that if our colour vocabulary were subject to the doubts raised by relevance scepticism we should not have a colour vocabularly, for we should be unable to satisfy minimal conditions for the existence of adequate criteria of application and use for the terms in such a vocabulary.

This thesis, once understood, appears trivially true. If the rules of a language assign the same name, with the same behaviour in discourse, to a given presentation irrespective of whether that presentation possesses a certain characteristic c, of a certain sort ϕ, or a quite different characteristic c' of the same sort, then that name is not a ϕ-name, although it may be the name 'ϕ'. And, equally clearly, if a language fails to discriminate between any c and any other c in the assignment of names then that language contains no names for determinates of ϕ, but, at most a single name for anything of that sort. But, if we are to be able to introduce a distinction between c and c' into our language it must be possible for us to formulate a rule of procedure which yields different results in discourse—generates different verbal material—according to whether we apply it to c or to c'. If we have such a procedure then discourse-neutral transposition is automatically ruled out. Such transposition requires a systematic relational symmetry between the objects of reference of names. But any procedure which discriminates characteristics of things for purpose of naming necessarily establishes asymmetrical relationships between the field of phenomena which it partitions into fields of application of names and the (generative) rules which accomplish the partitioning. The possibility of criteria of individuation for the most basic and fundamental objects of reference in our conceptual scheme is guaranteed, that is, not by the *chance* existence of asymmetries 'in nature', but by the fact that language, wherever it finds a foothold in our experience, must as a condition of finding such a foothold construct asymmetries which hold between the content of experience and the conventional procedures upon which the distinctions of reference enshrined in language are ultimately founded. And, by the same token, if the sceptic's arguments work then (as yet, and in the areas to which his arguments apply) we have no language: no conceptual vocabulary.

It is sometimes supposed that we can give meaning to a basic name by associating it with a characteristic context in which an experience of the sort referred to can be obtained, and some philosophers who think this also think that *all* basic names could in principle be replaced by such associations. On this view, 'x is red' means something like 'x is the colour of strawberries'. I shall call such expressions *contextual specifications*. It seems clear, now, that not all basic names could be replaced by contextual specifications, since at some point in a contextual specification we must identify the field of reference within which a particular presentation is being specified by giving a characteristic context of occurrence, and this task of idenification cannot, without a vicious regress, be performed by a further contextual specification. In the above example, for instance, the inclusion of the phrase 'the colour of' gives the game away.

I think we can go further than this, however, and argue that *no* basic experience term could be given a meaning by contextual specification. For a contextual specification, even when supplemented by the use of some general term like 'colour' whose meaning is antecedently known, gives us *only an instance of the correct use of* a term, T, and not a rule for *determining the limits of application of T*. In the absence of such a rule the referent of T remains unidentified, except in so far as T is identified as referring to *some* determination of the determinable denoted by the antecedently defined general term qualifying the contextual specification; but then T performs no linguistic function distinguishable from the function of that general term, and hence the operation of contextual specification which allegedly introduces it into the language in fact does no such thing: we have, in short, merely enacted an idle charade with no linguistic consequences whatsoever.[10]

Hence, it seems to me, the ultimate mechanisms which individuate the referents of basic experimental terms in a natural language can only be the ones described in the foregoing pages: contextual specification is at best a secondary mechanism which can serve on particular occasions to render more precise an inadequately developed conceptual vocabulary.

The situation in which we find ourselves according to the sceptic, now, is one in which both the following are true:

(i) we possess a perfectly functioning colour vocabulary within which we can apparently individuate as many objects of reference as we wish, depending on the degree of fineness of the mesh of discriminations which we choose to impose upon the colour array.

(ii) nevertheless, our ability to communicate by means of a common language is irrelevant to epistemological issues, and this irrelevance infects it in principle, and cannot be remedied, for example, by its further development in the direction of increasing fineness of the distinctions it allows.

If we are correct, (i) and (ii) cannot both be accurate descriptions of our condition, for we have shown that the possibility of formulating individuating criteria for the referents of colour

---

[10] How do children learn language if not by being taught the meanings of terms by what is, in effect, contexual specification? The answer, I think, is that they are not in this way being *taught meanings,* but merely given sample linguistic performances. Their task is then to find a *rule* which will enable them to generate such performances in a way consistent with adult usage. See my *Meaning and Structure, passim.*

names necessarily excludes the possibility of our being unable to detect transpositions of the fields of application of our common colour names in the experience of different observers. In order to specify a situation in which irresoluble epistemological difficulties concerning possible transposition of colours might arise, the sceptic would thus have to retreat to the postulation of a linguistic system which did *not* work smoothly; in which after a certain point, we found that we could not decrease the aperture of the mesh of discriminations which our language imposes upon the world. But first of all, we are plainly not in any such situation as regards colour, and secondly, even if we could be shown to be in such a situation with respect to any variety of sensory experience it is hard to see how we could be shown to be *necessarily* in it. For as we have seen, the provision of individuating criteria for objects of reference of basic experience terms does not depend merely upon good luck, or the lack of it, in possessing an experience exhibiting the right sort of relational asymmetry. The asymmetries upon which such individuating criteria ultimately rest depend not merely upon the phenomenology of our experience but upon our own ingenuity in inventing the generative procedures which operate on our experience to yield the limits of application and the behaviour in discourse of names. Red-green colour-blindness was difficult (though if Pickford is right about the use of compound names by the red-green blind, not impossible) to detect before the invention of appropriate testing procedures. But something more than present difficulty of detection was involved in the relevance-sceptic's position: he wished to claim a (quasi-) logical impossibility of detection.

IV

We are now left with the second form of relevance scepticism. Why should not Jones, instead of seeing exactly those colours which Smith sees, only transposed in some way, see a range of qualities quite different from any perceived by Smith, but related amongst themselves in exactly the ways in which the qualities which Smith calls 'colours' are related?

One or two preliminary constraints on this hypothesis need to be got clear. First, what can be meant by 'quite different'? It can only mean, I think, that the qualities in question would not be given, by Smith, any place in the colour array as he sees it, for any qualities given a place in that array would be, by that very fact, numbered among the colour presentations capable in principle of being seen by Smith. It follows that we cannot have intermediate sceptical hypotheses, in which Jones sees *some* of the colours seen by Smith, but with others of Smith's colours replaced by radically different *qualities having the same relationship to Jones' residual Smith-colours as the Smith-colours which Jones has lost;* the reason being that such hypotheses are incoherent. For a presentation to be placed next to a given shade of light blue in the colour array is just for it to *be* the next adjacent shade of light blue: for that is all that 'having the same relationship' to the first shade can consist in. What Jones call 'colours' then, are presentations which Smith would not call 'colours' at all, and neither perceives anything which the other calls a colour, but because the presentations which each calls 'colours' are related amongst themselves in exactly the same way as those which the other calls colours, discourse neutrality is preserved.

But for this proposal to be made intelligible we must be able to give a clear sense to the notion of two sets of presentations being internally related 'in the same way'; having 'the same' structure, 'the same' internal relationships. This is more difficult than might appear at first sight. 'x is the same as y' is unintelligible as it stands. To make it intelligible we must have an answer to the question 'the same in respect of what?'

To answer this question we must be able to identify, besides the concepts of x and y, some superordinate sortal concept under which both x and y fall. If we take, for example:

Arnold's face is the same colour as the wallpaper

what we say is intelligible because we can locate, besides the colour presentations exhibited by Arnold's face and the wallpaper, the concept 'colour' under which both colour presentations fall.

What, now are we to make of 'related in the same way'? Offhand it looks as if we can characterize identity of relationship in much the same way as we can characterize identity of properties, using the same range of ultimate superordinate concepts. Just as we can say:

x and y are the same colour
x is spatiotemporally identical with y

so it appears, we can say:

x and y are related in respect of colour in the same way as a and b
x, y and z are related in the same way as a, b and c in respect of their spatial configuration.

But matters become more complicated when we come to examine our ultimate sortal concepts themselves; for example, colour, pitch, numerical ratio, spatial configuration. If we have argued correctly, the possibility of forming the concept 'colour' depends upon our being able to single out, in our experience certain interrelated qualitative scales, or gradations of quality —the hue series, the tonality series and the saturation series— which in their interaction jointly constitute the colour array. The relationships between colour presentations which locate them relative to one another within the colour array, as Hume rightly observed, are not abstractable properties of colour presentations. Colour presentations are, in themselves, absolutely simple—to this extent Farrell is right to claim that they

are 'featureless'. But, by the same token, the relationships cannot be characterized as relationships of any *sort*, other than
colour itself.

It seems reasonable, now, to say that the members of two
sequences are colour presentations drawn from different sectors
of the colour array are each related among themselves 'in the
same way'. And moreover, it is because all the presentations
concerned are capable of being related to one another in this
way that they are all *colour* presentations. It looks, then, as if a
full explication of the notion of colour ought to require some
further account of what sort of relationships these are: an
account, in other words, which would satisfy the normal logical
requirement that assertions of identity must be qualified by
specifying the sortal in respect of which identity is being
predicated. But it seems impossible, for the reasons we have
just given, to give any answer to the question 'similarly related
in respect of what?' except 'in respect of colour (hue, tonality,
saturation)'. And this seems utterly uniformative, since the
relationships in question are themselves constitutive of the
notions which here allegedly function as superordinate concepts.

Does this mean that no explication can be given of the concept
of colour, or that the theory of colour naming that we have
developed has at length issued in circularity? I think not. We do
not need to be able to give any informative characterization of
the relationships which unite the colour array in order to be
able to recognize those relationships, and if we can recognize
them we can develop a vocabulary of colour names. And thus
we can explicate the concept by explaining the logic of colour
language, as we have in fact done in Part 3.

The implication of our inability to characterize colour relationships is, rather, this. To recognize something as coloured
is simply to place it within a series. The kind of series intended
can be *indicated*, by showing a set of colour presentations
arranged so as to form a series of the requisite sort, but it can-

not be verbally characterized. At the point where we ask some-one to continue a series of gradations of hue, or degrees of tonality or saturation we can only rely upon what Wittgenstein calls 'a shared pattern of response'. If somebody selects an appropriate colour presentation to continue the series, well and good: he has grasped the notion of hue, or saturation, or whatnot. And if he does not select an appropriate colour presentation he has not grasped the notion, and very little else can be done to explain it to him: perhaps he does not see colours as we see them. It seems then that the most enlightening account we can give of the meaning of 'coloured' is to say that a thing is coloured just in case it can be assigned to a place in the colour array.

Let us now return to the radical sceptic. His problem is to characterize the respect in which the relationships linking the presentations which comprise Jones' colour universe are 'the same as' those linking the presentations comprising Smith's colour universe. The most promising mode of characterization might seem to be one which appeals directly to conformity of linguistic usage. We might thus try the following formulation. 'Smith's and Jones' colour arrays exhibit systems of internal relationships which are the same in their effects upon Smith's and Jones' respective use of colour names.'

This, however, will not do. What the sceptic is trying to show is that it is possible for two arrays of presentations to be similarly internally structured in such a way as to yield indistinguishable patterns of use of language. The above formulation does not *show* this to be possible, it simply asserts it to be possible. What we need from the sceptic is a characterization of the relationships uniting the colour array which is such as to make it clear that a set of qualitatively quite different presentations might exhibit internal relationships which would be 'the same' in a sense conformable to the sceptic's purpose. To by-pass this demand by appealing directly to conformity of usage as a way of explaining his sense of 'the same' gets him nowhere.

What makes the rules of our language generate the linguistic performances that they do generate is simply the internal relational structure of the colour array. If the sceptic's radically disparate array leads Jones to talk about colour in ways indistinguishable from Smith's, this can only be, indeed, because the internal structure of the sceptic's postulated array is the same as that of the colour array. But now we are back to the question 'the same in what respect?' To clinch his case the sceptic needs to show that the internal relational structure of the colour array could be filled in by a quite different content: that content can be imagined varying while structure is held steady. To do this he needs to be able to specify clearly what exactly it is that we are to imagine being held steady while content changes, and to give such a specification is, of course, to specify the respects in which the structure of the two arrays are 'the same' in some way which makes no reference to the conformity of linguistic usage which is supposed to result from the kind of identity which is at issue.

To characterize two things as the same in some respect we need, as we have already argued, some superordinate concept by reference to which the respect in question can be identified and under which the things in question can be shown to fall in some way. Thus if six objects are arranged to form two triangles, the identification of the respect in which the two groups are similar must proceed by reference to the general concept of triangularity and beyond that to the whole fabric of our conceptual scheme so far as it concerns spatial relationship.

If the sceptic is to be able to characterize his sense of 'related in the same way' he must, then, be able to indicate some superordinate concept, which can be shown in some way to apply to both the colour array and the sceptic's postulated array, and which serves to identify the kind of structural identity which the sceptic wishes to postulate. It follows that, if the sceptic is correct, the colour array and his postulated array will each exemplify some sortal concept of greater generality than the concept 'colour'.

What kind of concept, now, could this be? It is true, of course, that we do possess some sortal concepts of greater generality than the concept 'colour'. These include, for example, 'sensory modality', 'feature of experience', 'type of quality' and 'existent'. None of these will serve the sceptic's purpose, for a very good reason. None of them serves to identify any feature either of content or structure, which colours in general possess in common with other sorts of thing. Such concepts indeed seem curiously vacuous. The source of their vacuity, I think, is that they are not themselves sortal concepts at all but expressions for referring in general terms to genuine sortals. None of them, that is, corresponds to a rule or principle for dividing the world into things which are of a certain sort and things which are not. Rather, each of them serves as a verbal device for referring to *any* division of the world that might be accomplished by genuine sortal concepts. Their vacuity is a result of their unlimited generality.

If the only superordinate concept which a given concept falls under is a dummy sortal of this kind, then the concept in question is basic or ultimate in our conceptual scheme. And this is confirmed by the fact that it is impossible to characterize the relationships which unite the colour array or the qualitative contents which possess these relationships except—uninformatively—as 'colours' or 'colour relations'. But if such characterization is impossible then the sceptic's demand for a genuine sortal concept under which both the colour array and his postulated array fall is doomed to disappointment.

It might be thought that the nature of the requisite sortal concept would become clear if we had sensory access to both the colour array and the sceptic's postulated array: for then, perhaps, we could abstract the requisite concept by comparing the two arrays. This suggestion is naïve. It rests on the supposition that we form concepts simply by noticing similarities in nature, so that with such a similarity before my eyes, as it were, I have access to a given concept, while without it I have no means of formulating the concept of all. But a concept is something more than an observed similarity. It is a rule or principle for distinguishing, or separating off, *sorts* or *kinds* of thing (in a vacuously general sense of 'thing') within the general fabric of our experience. If it were possible to formulate a concept by means of which the *kind* of relations which subsist between colour presentations could be specified informatively, in such a way as to make it clear how such relations could be represented as an adequately defined formal schema capable of being filled by qualitatively different contents, we could do it by reference to the colour array alone.

But, as we have seen, the relationships in question can be specified only (uninformatively) as the relationships which colour presentations stand in to one another. The concept of colour is ultimate in our conceptual scheme. There is no further conceptual level at which the content and the interrelationships of colour presentations might be prised apart. And hence they cannot be prised apart. The form of the colour array is uniquely related to its content, or to put it more accurately, form and content form a logically indissoluble unity, upon which the sceptic's attempts to formulate his alternative possibilities can find no purchase.

To this the sceptic might retort that if we can speak of different sets of colour presentations, drawn from different sectors of the colour array, as exhibiting interrelationships of the same general sort, there is no reason why he should not talk in the same way about sets of presentations drawn respectively from the colour array and from his postulated array. This is fair enough, as long as he is prepared to meet the logical preconditions of such talk. The reason we are able to predicate similarity of the relationships uniting sets of presentations drawn from different sectors of the colour array is, as we have seen, that the colour array is one continuous system of internal relationships. For the sceptic to be able to make the move which he is at present contemplating he must, therefore, allow continuity of the same sort to hold between his postulated array and the colour array. But this makes his claim openly self-contradictory, for now he is claiming both that his array is qualitatively radically disparate from the colour array, and that it is at the same time qualitatively continuous with it.

V

What we have just been saying sounds, I suppose, vaguely reminiscent of F. H. Bradley's criticisms of 'relational thought'. We have been saying in effect that the relationships which unite colour presentations into an array can only be specified by reference to colour presentations themselves (i.e. to certain contents), while colour presentations in turn can only be specified by reference to the relationships in which they stand to one another. If I can speak about 'a slightly greenish shade of light blue' or 'the relation of increasing darkness displayed by these three reds', it is only by courtesy of a constant conceptual shuttling back and forth between things and their relations. No doubt this is part of what philosophers have meant by characterizing colour relationships as 'internal'. And yet there is something odd and circular about the whole performance. Ordinary specification of particulars and properties does not proceed in closed loops. If I specify my door as 'the only door painted green on the first floor of stage A of the Arts Building at the University of Sussex', I do not need to be acquainted with the particular door in question, or any set of doors, to grasp the nature of the relationships in which my door is here being described as standing to things of other kinds. And this has something to do with the fact that the relations in question are, in traditional terms, mainly external ones. Why then, should our conceptual scheme contain closed loops at all? I think there is a reason, and to uncover it will make it very much clearer what sort of refutation of radical scepticism I am proposing, and why the refutation works.

First let us notice that our experience presents us with other sets of internally related particulars[11] besides colour presentations. For example, sounds are continuously internally related in pitch, and in terms of various kinds of tonal or modal scales ('note' and 'sound' stand in a relationship reminiscent of that holding between 'colour' and 'colour presentation'). Space itself is an order of internal relationships, as is number.

What enables me to recognize that middle c played on a piano (hereafter referred to as c) is not a colour? Obscurely daft though this question may seem, it has a perfectly sensible answer. This is that c does not fit at any point into the colour array. It does not fit more appropriately between any two colour presentations than between any two others, which is no more than to say that it has no place at all on the colour array.

What divides the world up for me into things of radically different logical type (sounds, musical notes, colours, numbers, volumes of space) is, then, solely the fact that systems of internal relations—closed loops—such as the colour array exist. Such a system determines the membership of the logical category which it dominates simply by not accepting things of other category as items within the system. It defines by rejecting. The limits of a logical category of objects are simply the limits of a certain mode of internal relationship.

Let us now suppose for the sake of argument that no such systems of internal relations existed, and that our experience presented us solely with external relationships. If this were the case the assertion that c does not fit into the colour array would

[11] I realize that I am here using 'particular' in an idiosyncratic sense, in which it does not contrast with 'universal'. I am forced to use it in this way by the lack of a suitable alternative term ('feature' might do, but carries certain unwelcome connotations, as do 'object' and 'individual'). What I intend by it is, I think, always clear from the context, so that it *should* cause no confusion.

be a contingent assertion. It would follow from this that it would be logically possible for c to fit into the colour array, and only contingently the case that it could not be fitted in, perhaps because not all the colours which we might under different circumstances perceive were (on account of some practical defect or deficiency perceived by us.

But now we are moving in a circle. If c *might* fit into the colour array, then it must stand in internal relations to colour presentations; and thus the colour array and the array of sounds form one continuous array. And thus if we apply the same arguments to other logical categories of objects, we shall end with a universe somewhat reminiscent of Bradley's,[12] consisting of one vast array of internal relations. And clearly in such a universe there would be no possibility of asserting contingent propositions, because there would be no external relations.

It looks, then, as though the supposition that the universe might exhibit only external relations is self-defeating. But no doubt this is only because we have not examined the implications of that possibility closely enough. We have assumed that, under this hypothesis, our experience would continue to be divisible into categories of objects—colours, sounds, spatial volumes and so on. But if we keep these familiar categories we keep internal relations as well. We must therefore abandon this assumption if we want to see what an experience characterized solely by external relations would be like.

But now our description of experience looks very odd indeed. We can no longer divide experience into logically separate categories of object. There is thus only one kind of object, and objects of this kind stand only in external relationships to one another. It now becomes difficult to see how, in such a universe, I could identify particular objects for the purpose of making contingent assertions. I could not identify them by contrasting their logical category with that of other objects ('the *colour* filling

[12] But not, of course, the same as Bradley's. Bradley's Absolute is not an array of internal relations.

that *shape*', e.g.), for categorial distinctions are no longer available. Even to admit space and time into our universe would admit distinct logical categories (points, volumes of space, e.g. and correlative systems of internal relations; for I presume that the objects postulated by the hypothesis are not defined in spatial terms, for otherwise they would not be only externally related.

It seems to me in short that upon the hypothesis that our experience contains only external relationships, the possibility of contingent assertion is ruled out. The possibility of asserting contingent propositions, and the existence of logically distinct categories of object are necessarily bound up together.

It is not difficult to see why this should be so. A proposition is contingent just in case we can *independently* identify what is being said, and what it is being said about. Consider, for example,

My door is four inches wider than yours.

This is a contingent proposition, and what makes it contingent is that it is possible to identify doors *as* doors, and to identify particular doors by their owners, independently of any considerations concerning their width or other dimensions. And similarly, I can give a rule for determining relative lengths without mentioning either doors or the conventions which assign rooms in a university building to their owners. And I can apply this rule equally well either to doors or to any of a wide range of other sorts of thing. Contingent assertion thus requires that it should be possible to specify relationships in which things of many different sorts can stand to one another. Such relationships are, of course, external, in the sense that they can be specified without the necessity of mentioning any specific set of objects between which they hold. And most of the time, when we describe the ways in which things are related in the world, we are talking about relationships of this kind.

Not all predicates and particulars can be independently specifiable, however, if any are to be. For we shall eventually reach a point in constructing our conceptual scheme at which we have to specify the ultimate sorts of particular and the ultimate sorts of predicate in terms of which contingent propositions are framed. We shall have to pass from *using* the concepts of a door, of linear dimensions, of redness, in other words, to establishing the limits of the concept of colour, of a material object, of number.

If objects corresponding to these ultimate sortal concepts were presented to us as part of 'the given'—if our experience 'came' ready-divided into natural nameables of the requisite sort—there would be no problem. We could simply associate names with these nameables on a one-to-one basis. As we have seen in the case of colour, and as I think is sufficiently obvious in the case of a great many other very general sortal concepts, our experience is not presented to us as a fabric of natural nameables of the requisite sort. The concepts in question have to be constructed. Now, any such process of construction will involve, in very general terms, locating objects of reference through their relationships. This is perhaps obvious in the case of clearly 'structural' concepts such as those of number, or spatial location, or of a note in music; and I have tried to show that it is also true of colour. But now the relationships in question cannot be external—cannot, that is, be relationships *in which a number of different sorts of objects might equally well stand to one another*— since if they were they would simply not be of any use to us as a means of defining the *sort*—the logical category of objects in question; and the problem of defining ultimate kinds would simply be pushed back a step. If colour relations could hold between material objects, or volumes of space, or musical notes, as well as between colour presentations we could not define the logical category of colour by reference to them.

In short, then, the possibility of independently identifying particulars and their predicates and relationships, in order to

frame contingent assertions, only exists because at an ultimate
level in our conceptual scheme our experience can be divided
sharply and exclusively into distinct logical categories, each
of which allows a vocabulary of concepts to be defined within
the limits of that category, and so independently of parallel
processes of conceptual construction going on in other categories.

Thus, in order for independent specification of particulars
and predicates, and thus for the assertion of contingent propositions, to exist at lower levels in our conceptual scheme, that
scheme at its highest level must terminate in the closed loops
of mutually defined and defining objects and relationships
which correspond to our most general sortal concepts.

In a curious way, then, the radical sceptic is hoist with his
own petard. He chooses, for obvious reasons, to operate at the
extreme limits of our conceptual scheme. This is because, at
lower levels, the doubts we experience seem capable of resolu-
tion. I may wonder if a fish seen under water, or the face of
my neighbour in the bus queue seen under sodium-vapour
streetlighting, is really the colour it appears to be, but my
doubts can be resolved when I bring the fish to the surface or
my neighbour and I get on the bus. The irresoluble doubts
characteristic of philosophical scepticism only become formul-
able when we approach the limits of our conceptual scheme.
Does 'red' mean the same thing to you as it does to me? Does
'colour'? The trouble is now, that the sceptic's arguments
depend upon postulating different terms standing in the same
relationship to one another. At lower levels in our conceptual
scheme such postulations are not only possible but the stuff of
everyday discourse. (Could the sofa stand in the same relation
as the piano does now to the fireplace and the far wall? Of
course.) But at the ultimate level at which the sceptic chooses
to operate they are not. The relationships which subsist between
colour presentations could not subsist between things of another
sort. They exist at all merely because colour presentations

have the qualitative character that they have. Such unique linkages between term and relation must exist in our experience if
we are to be able to divide the world into independently specifiable families of concepts; and the sceptic, unfortunately for
him, has chosen to postulate alternatives just at the point where
the postulation of alternatives is, as it must be somewhere or
other, logically out of place. To be incapable of being placed
on the colour array as we perceive it is simply to be not a
colour, and thus not capable of standing as a term in colour
relationships. And that is the end of the matter. The sceptic has
stepped, not into a conceivable alternative perceptual universe,
but into a logical void.

VI

My general point can be put in another way, I have been
arguing that the linguistic and conceptual machinery which
governs colour naming works in such a way that any difference
in the perceived content of the colour presentations seen by
different speakers must show itself in differences in the way
in which they apply colour names, or in the privileges of occurrence in sentential contexts which colour names display in their
discourse.

Now, patterns of applications of names, or privileges of
occurrence, are *formal structures*. That is, they can be described
without mentioning colour contents. And, as we have seen, it
is tempting to suppose that *these* are the structures—the array of
relationships specifiable independently of reference to colour
contents—which the sceptic needs in order to formulate his
hypothesis about alternative colour universes.

The trouble with this is that these relationships hold between
words and other words, or between words and their circumstances of utterance. There is a crucial distinction, which I tried
to get clear throughout the earlier part of this book, between

the structure of language and the structure of the world, or of experience. The sceptic can only treat logical grammar, or patterns of application of names, as supplying the specification he requires of the 'formal' element of colour experience, at the cost of ignoring this distinction. For what the sceptic needs in reality is some way of specifying the relationships which hold between colour presentations, and of doing so without mentioning the colour presentations between which they hold in our ordinary perceptual universe. And these are not relationships holding between elements of language, or between elements of language and elements of the world.

But now it might be argued that this is, after all, not a difficult demand. The relationships in question are simply *similarity relationships*, and an alternative set of colour presentations will be structurally isomorphous with the 'ordinary' set (for 'ordinary', if the sceptic's argument succeeds must be put in inverted commas—my 'ordinary' set might not be yours!) in the required sense just in case it contains presentations which can be arranged in sequence by reference to degree of relative similarity.

This move is, in a way, shrewd enough. For all that our experience presents us with, so far as colour is concerned, is an array of presentations which can be ordered in certain ways on considerations of differential relative similarity. One might almost say that we are *given* only the colour presentations, and that the relationships between them, about which we have had so much to say, are in reality nothing over and above the bare presentations themselves (and I think this is in a way true, if it is taken as no more than a way of saying that the relationships cannot be independently specified).

Again, if our argument in Part 3 is broadly correct, the whole logical grammar of colour names, and their patterns of application, flow from (are generated by operations which involve) the carrying-out of linguistic procedures which all, in the end, amount merely to complex reiterations of the single operation of checking by inspection the degree of relative similarity of three or more colour presentations, and acting in various ways depending upon the outcome of the inspection. It therefore seems all the more reasonable to suppose that the structural isomorphy which the sceptic requires can be specified simply as 'a similar disposition of relationships of relative similarity' or some such formula.

Alas. The sceptic's old troubles over specifying the *type* of similarity he has in mind arise reinvigorated in connexion with the first 'similar' in this formula. Colour is not the only sensory modality in which unanalysable similarities are to be found. Sounds (or Aural Presentations if the pedantic impulse is allowed its head) similarly admit of being classed as relatively more or less resemblant in respect of pitch, timbre and other qualities. The crucial point, now, is that *these* relationships of relative similarity determine a radically different logical grammar from that determined by the sort of relative-similarity relationships that subsist between colour presentations. For example, one cannot speak of one colour presentation as being 'one octave above' another, and many other such examples will suggest themselves on a moment's reflection.

The sceptic, therefore, needs to be able to specify what *kind* of relationships of relative similarity subsist between colour presentations, and, for example, how *this* kind of relative-similarity relationship differs from the kind of relative-similarity relationships which subsist between sounds. Only if he can do *this* can he adequately specify the constitution of his alternative perceptual universe.

Here, now I think, we have the sceptic penned up against a wall. The wall in question marks the limit of our conceptual scheme. Without such a limit, as we have seen, we should not have a conceptual scheme.

If we now ask ourselves *what accounts for* the peculiar logical grammar of colour names, as distinct from that of talk about sound, for example, we can give two answers. On one level, the answer is, of course, the nature of the linguistic procedures which constitute the concepts of 'red', 'pink', 'colour' and so on. But these procedures themselves can only be specified—in teaching them to someone, for example—by reference to the nature of our experience of colour. It seems, then, that we must say that what in the end accounts for both the possibility of specifying the procedures constitutive of colour concepts, and the logical grammar of these concepts, is the bare qualitative character of our colour experience itself: not its form but its content. Form, then, is not something which can be abstracted, even in thought, from content, content itself being dismissed as 'featureless'. 'Form', where in that term we can include both the relational structure of the colour array and the entire linguistic fabric of constitutive procedures and logical grammar erected upon the basis of that structure, is itself a complex feature of content, Hence, if we suppose Jones' colour experience to be radically different from Smith's in its qualitative content from Smith's we necessarily suppose its 'form' in this broad sense, to be radically different as well.

My general conclusion, then, is this. It is a perfectly reasonable supposition that beings with differently constituted sense organs might experience sensory presentations different from any that we experience. It is not a reasonable supposition that such presentations might be 'formally' indistinguishable from colours. Such a supposition is not unreasonable because there are practical reasons for supposing that such isomorphy would never occur in nature. It is unreasonable because it cannot be formulated without lapsing into logical incoherence.

VII

I am pretty sure that many of my readers, even if they sympathize with the general line I am pursuing, will feel a certain uneasiness at this point. If I am right they will be feeling a haunting sense that, despite all argument, the sceptic has a point. Perhaps some other set of presentations *could* be structured in the same way as the colour array. Perhaps even now, behind the eyes of my Aunt Amy, or the Vice-Chancellor, an exotic jungle of alternative colours is blooming in the foreign soil of another mind.

To entertain this doubt, however, is to suppose that the concept of colour and the concept of the type of relationship which unites the colour array are two logically distinct concepts, specifiable independently of one another. For if the doubt in question is a logically conceivable one, then that type of relationship must be capable of being exemplified by quite different sorts of object, and cannot therefore be logically tied through its specification to one. And by the same token, what makes something a colour must be specifiable without mentioning the relationships in question, for if things of another sort can equally well stand to one another in those relationships, the possibility of standing in them cannot be constitutive of the concept of colour.

In entertaining the sceptic's hypothesis, that is, we are tricking ourselves into the covert assumption that colour relationships are external relationships, which is precisely what the sceptic wishes us to do.

One thing which makes such self-deception easy is the acceptance of an associative theory of naming. If we can think of 'red', or any other colour name, as definable in isolation from other colour names by the ostensive indication of suitably chosen samples, then it becomes easy to think of 'colour' as definable in much the same way. Our conceptual scheme may then appear as an array of independently specifiable name-referent linkages, so that it becomes easy to make the further assumption that all the relationships linking the referents in question are external ones.

It is a philosophical commonplace, derived from the later work of Wittgenstein, that explanations must end somewhere'.

This gnomic apophthegm is sometimes made to serve as an argument against scepticism. Explanations of concepts must come to an end at some point, it is argued, and the sceptic's error consists precisely in the fact that he wishes to go on indefinitely raising doubts beyond the point at which he must give up such philosophical luxuries, accepting some notions in our conceptual scheme as primitive and beyond question as the price of constructing any conceptual scheme at all. Unfortunately, as we can now see, if the points at which explanation is supposed to end are taken to be associative linkages between names and natural nameables, as they very often are, this argument against scepticism has no force whatsoever.

On the other hand, if the points at which explanation must stop, at which we must rely, in Wittgenstein's terms 'on a shared response', are points at which what must be grasped is not an associative linkage but a necessary relationship between an object's being of a certain sort, and its standing in certain kinds of relationship to other objects of that sort, then, as I have tried to show, the remark that 'explanation must end somewhere' has genuine force against even the most radical type of scepticism.

To take this view is, of course, to treat our conceptual scheme not as an extensional but as an intensional structure, but then there are plenty of other reasons for supposing that the logic of a natural language cannot be an extensional logic.

Recognizing this, we can now see more clearly some of the merits of Wittgenstein's position in the *Tractatus*, and of at least some of Schlick's position in *Form and Content*. The privileges of occurrences of words in discourse are indeed, in a sense, determined by systems of internal relationships. But the relationships in question do not hold between the members of a single class of metaphysically ultimate simples, construed as the referents of basic names. They are relationships of radically different kinds and they hold between radically different sorts of things. In the case of colour they hold between colour presentations. But colour presentations are not the same thing as colours, which are the real referents of colour names. And the internal relationships that link colour presentations are not, as we saw in discussing Schlick, relationships of possibility of combination in states of affairs.

Logical grammar is the outcome not just of internal relationships within the fabric of the Real, but of systems of rules which operate in part upon those relationships and generate linguistic performances. Which sentences make sense and which do not is determined in the end by the possibilities of operating such systems of rules in conjunction with one another. The sense of a sentence such as 'My door is green' is guaranteed by the fact that the rules which establish the meaning of 'door' incidentally locate extended surfaces. And that something should possess a surface is a sufficient precondition for its being coloured. 'My door is iambic' fails as a would-be meaningful sentence because we can completely specify the notion of a door without in the process locating anything which satisfies minimal conditions for the ascription of the term 'iambic', given the nature of the rules which confer meaning upon that term. (Unless, of course, we are using 'iambic' in an extended sense—whereby hangs another and even longer tale.)

To reduce logical grammar to a set of internal properties of basic objects of reference, thereby assimilating the structure of language lock, stock and barrel, as it were, to the structure of the world, is the result of combining correct insights concerning the creativity and originality of language use with an associative-referential theory of meaning. Once this assimilation is made, a distinction between what can be said and what can only be shown is a necessary consequence. We can afford to dispense with the distinction in its full-blooded Tractarian form; but we are left with a rump version of the distinction. If we are right, nothing can be *said* about the nature of the relationships linking colour presentations. They cannot be characterized, they can only be indicated, or in Wittgenstein's terms, *shown*, by the workings of language.

VIII

It remains to clear up one or two residual questions. First, it might be objected that we have all along assumed that the colour array is something public; that it is 'out there'. And yet surely a colour presentation is a paradigm case of a secondary quality. Colours would have no existence if there were no conscious minds to perceive them. The experience of perceiving a colour has been used by philosophers, from Descartes to Moore, as a prime example of a mental state. And hence, surely, a colour is something essentially private: something that comes into being only when neural impulses from the retina enter that sealed an inaccessible central cell of the neurological telephone exchange known as the mind.

It is precisely this familiar complex of persuasive pictures of the way things are that I have been trying, in a small way and in certain directions only, to subvert.

What I have been saying is that colours are public, and not private, at least to the extent that we can talk about them with a logically unassailable assurance that we are talking about (qualitatively) the same things—colour-blindness and other detectable differences in colour vision apart.

Experiences of colour are indeed conscious states. This means that, if our argument is sound, what you say about colours, given that it is not merely learned by rote and parroted, or generated by a series of mnemonic rules having nothing intrinsically to do with colour (such as that roses are red and violets are blue), can give me a logically adequate assurance both that you are indeed experiencing conscious mental states and that the states in question are of a certain qualitative character. I cannot, of course, see into your mind or think your thoughts, but I can know that you are seeing something that appears coloured, and—colour-blindness apart—what colour it appears to you. And I can know these things because you can tell them to me. And so, if we have argued successfully, we have achieved all that philosophy can never hope to achieve, which is to arrive after long struggles at the commonplace.

Appendix

It has been suggested to me that 'colour' could be defined in terms of external relationships. Colours, for example, are determinations of surfaces, but are imperceptible to touch. They are *visual* properties. They are invariant, within limits, with respect to changes in texture or shape; and variable, within limits, with respect to changes in lighting or juxtaposition with other colours; and so on.

People who accept the possibility of such a definition generally do so, I think, because they are convinced by Wittgenstein's arguments against the idea that any set of words might be given a meaning by 'private' acts of ostensive definition. They wish to emphasise the existence of connexions between the concepts of seemingly 'private' entities—immediate sensory presentations, mental states and acts of one sort or another—and public, behavioural criteria of reference. This desire is unexceptionable, but it has nothing to do with the question of whether the relationships ultimately constitutive of a given concept are internal or external. The account of colour concepts which I have given here ties them just as firmly to public behavioural criteria of use and reference, and secures their 'publicity' as effectively, as an account of the sort offered above without the disadvantage of allowing a distinction between form and content, with its attendant sceptical consequences, to get off the ground. The fact that I am prepared to allow the possibility of public identifying reference to something as suspiciously 'mental' as the content of an experience of colour does not make me, as a Marxist friend complained recently in conversation, a subjective idealist.

The main objection to regarding external relations as constitutive of the concept 'colour' is that, *pace* Locke, a complex property is not the same thing as a heap, or aggregate, of (nominally) simpler properties. It might be possible to compile a list of external properties of the sort suggested above, such that all colour presentations, and only colour presentations, would possess all the properties on the list. But then we should have no way of explaining why, when it came to forming complex concepts, we should be interested in the list composed by just *these* properties, and not some other list composed, say, by half the properties in question. The obvious answer is that this list happens to single out all, and only, colours. But then, what are colours? Why do colours possess the unity proper to a single category of objects, grouped under a single concept? A theory couched in terms of external properties is silent on this point. So we must look elsewhere for a principle of unity, which, after all, is what an account of the constitution of a concept is supposed to offer us.

Index